100 VENISON *Recipes*

100 VENISON Recipes

From Down Home to Uptown

HENRY SINKUS

⧉ WILLOW CREEK PRESS®

Published by Willow Creek Press
P.O. Box 147, Minocqua, Wisconsin 54548

For information on other Willow Creek Press titles,
call 1-800-850-9453

Library of Congress Cataloging-in-Publication Data: On File

Printed in The United States of America

TABLE OF CONTENTS

SOUPS, CHILIES & CHOWDERS 13

VENISON SOUP 14

LEFTOVER VENISON ROAST SOUP 15

THAI VENISON SHANK SOUP 16

GOULASH SOUP 18

HOT CHILI 19

SPICY VENISON AND CORN CHOWDER 20

VENISON CHILI WITH CHORIZO SAUSAGE 21

VENISON CHILI WITH ITALIAN SAUSAGE 22

STEWS & CASSEROLES 25

AUSSIE MARINATED VENISON 26

SOUTHWESTERN CASSEROLE 27

CAMP STEW 28

VENISON AND WILD RICE GUMBO 30

HUNTING CAMP ITALIAN CASSEROLE 31

MASHED POTATO, VENISON AND SPINACH PIE 32

MOROCCAN STEW 34

MOTHER MARY'S VENISON STEW 35

MUSTARD HERB VENISON 36

TEXAS VENISON AND BEANS 37

SPANISH RAGOUT OF VENISON 38

VENISON BURGANDY 40

VENISON STEW PARNASSUS 41

VENISON STEW WITH SQUASH 42

VENISON STEW 43

BERLINER VENISON AND SAUERKRAUT 44

BASQUE STEW 45

STEAKS, ROASTS & CHOPS 47

BAYOU VENISON 48

BREADED VENISON CHOPS 49

BBQ VENISON CHOPS WITH WILD RICE PANCAKES 50

CAROLINA BBQ 52

CHICKEN FRIED VENISON STEAK 54

STEAK AU POIVRE 56

LEMON VENISON CHOPS 57

POT-AU-FEU FOR TWO 58

RHEINISCHER STUFFED VENISON ROAST 60

WARSAW VENISON 61

ROAST VENISON WITH APRICOTS, PRUNES AND PEARS 62

SAUERBRATEN 64

VENISON SCHNITZEL 66

SOUTH OF THE BORDER VENISON 67

CORIANDER AND HONEY GLAZED VENISON CHOPS 68

SZECHUAN VENISON WITH DRIED CRANBERRIES IN PORT WINE 69

THAI CURRY 70

TERIYAKI VENISON 71

VENISON CHOPS AND SAUSAGE WITH SAUERKRAUT 72

VENISON SHOULDER ROAST WITH APPLES, TURNIPS & CARROTS 73

VENISON PICCATA 74

NEW ENGLAND VENISON ROAST 75

VENISON WITH PEPPERS AND PASTA 76

VENISON WITH PEPPERS AND PEA PODS 77

VENISON ROULADEN 78

VENISON, VERY DRY WITH AN OLIVE 79

VENISON WITH ZINFANDEL AND DRIED CRANBERRIES 80

ROAST VENISON LOIN A LA FRANKFURT 82

VENISON MEDALLIONS WITH PORT WINE AND LINGONBERRIES 83

VENISON FAJITAS 84

HUNGARIAN VENISON PAPRIKASH 85

MEDITERRANEAN VENISON 86

VENISON STROGANOFF 87

VENISON SHOULDER ROAST WITH BREAD STUFFING 88

GROUND VENISON 91

BREAKFAST SKILLET 92

VENISON BREAKFAST WRAP 93

BURGERS WITH BACON AND CHEDDAR CHEESE 94

GERMAN STYLE GROUND VENISON 95

FRITTATA 96

INDIVIDUAL MEATLOAVES 98

ITALIAN MEATBALLS 99

KONIGSBERGER KLOPSE (GERMAN MEATBALLS) 100

MEATLOAF A LA REUBEN 102

MEATLOAF 103

MOSTACIOLLI 104

QUICK STROGANOFF 105

RAGOUT 106

SPAGHETTI SAUCE 107

SPICY VENISON AND EGGPLANT 108

STUFFED BURGERS 109

VENISON TURBAN 110

STUFFED PEPPERS 112

SWEET SOUR STUFFED CABBAGE 113

THAI COUNTRY-STYLE CURRY 114

THAI MEATBALLS 115

VENISON AND SPANISH RICE 116

VENISON BBQ 117

VENISON AND CORNBREAD PIE 118

VENISON DUMPLINGS BOLOGNESE 120

VENISON POCKET 121

VENISON WITH BLACKBEANS AND RICE 122

VENISON QUATTRO FORMAGGIO 123

STUFFED ACORN SQUASH 124

MISCELLANEOUS VENISON RECIPES 127

CACCIATORE 128

FARMHOUSE VENISON 129

FINNISH VENISON AND PORK 130

SATÉ 131

RACK OF VENISON 132

SWEET SOUR VENISON 133

VENISON BROCCOLI STIR-FRY 134

VENISON CURRY 135

ITALIAN VENISON CUTLETS WITH ARTICHOKE HEARTS 136

INDEX 139

INTRODUCTION

Venison is one of the most heart-healthy red meats and is available from specialty markets, on the internet and as the product of the successful hunt. This book showcases venison's versatility and is organized into two sections—Down Home and Uptown.

The Down Home recipes are traditional comfort foods, dishes that you would most likely prepare for your family. The Uptown recipes are for those special evenings when you want to impress business associates, the new neighbors or old friends.

Over half of the recipes in this book can be prepared in 60 minutes or less and all will have your family and friends asking for more and wondering how you manage to produce such wonderful dishes.

My wife, Mary, and I own and operate the Pine Baron's Restaurant and Custom Catering Service in Manitowish Waters, Wisconsin. In my previous life, I worked for large corporations and traveled extensively. I experienced firsthand, products from many lands and cooking techniques from various cultures. Our menu at the restaurant is as diversified as the recipes in this book. I think of my kitchen as an art studio and my spice rack as a paint palate. Let your own creative juices flow—as you find your favorite recipes here, add your own special touches—spice it up a little, add a different herb, use a different meat, pair it with a bottle of wine from your favorite vineyard, serve it with your favorite side dish— the possibilities are endless. But most importantly, enjoy. And don't forget to add a large dose of love!

Would you prepare fish the same you cook pork? Why do so many cook venison the way they cook beef? Venison is one of the most heart-healthy and versatile red meats available and should be served to both family and guests.

-Henry Sinkus

LEGEND

| UPTOWN RECIPES | DOWN HOME RECIPES | DIFFICULTLY (1-5) |

THROUGHOUT THE BOOK YOU WILL SEE THE ICONS ABOVE.

*UPTOWN RECIPES ARE DENOTED WITH A WINE GLASS.

*DOWN HOME RECIPES ARE DENOTED WITH A BEER MUG.

* THE FORK METER INDICATES RECIPE DIFFICULTY BASED

ON TIME AND/OR TECHNIQUE.

SOUPS, CHILIES & CHOWDERS

VENISON SOUP

SERVES 6–8

INGREDIENTS

- 2 lbs. venison shank cut into 1–2" slices
- 1 8-oz. boneless, skinless chicken breast, diced
- 3 or 4 slices bacon, cooked and crumbled
- 1 large onion, diced
- 2 medium carrots, sliced and quartered
- 1 parsnip, sliced and quartered
- 4–5 stalks celery, sliced
- 3 tbsp. fresh parsley, chopped
- Olive oil
- 6–8 peppercorns
- 8 cups water and 3 tbsp. low-salt chicken base
- 3 egg yolks
- ½ cup heavy cream mixed with ½ cups sour cream

SERVE WITH A LOAF OF THICK-CRUSTED BREAD FOR THE PERFECT FALL OR WINTER DINNER.

DIRECTIONS

In a heavy stockpot, brown the venison in olive oil and remove to a microwavable dish. Sauté the onion, celery, carrot and parsnip in the stockpot until tender—add olive oil if necessary.

Cover the microwavable dish with plastic wrap and microwave on high for 6 minutes. Microwave for additional minutes until the meat separates from the bone. Remove the venison from the bones. Place the bones and any liquid in the stockpot. Add the peppercorns. Stir in the water and chicken base. Simmer on low for 2–3 hours. Strain the stock, heat to a boil and add the chicken breast. Reduce heat to simmer. Cut the venison into bite-size pieces and add to the stock. Simmer for 30 minutes.

Blend the egg yolks with the cream mixture. Slowly add 2 cups of the hot stock to this mixture, stirring vigorously. Slowly add this mixture to the hot stock, stirring constantly to prevent curdling. Adjust seasonings. Garnish with fresh chopped parsley and crumbled bacon.

LEFTOVER VENISON ROAST SOUP

INGREDIENTS

- 3–4 cups cooked venison roast, sliced ¼" thick and cut into ½" wide strips
- 1 tbsp. minced garlic
- 1 large onion, peeled, sliced and quartered
- 2 medium potatoes, peeled and cut into ½" dice
- 3 stalks celery, sliced
- 4 carrots, peeled, sliced ½" thick and cut in half
- 2 tbsp. olive oil
- 2 qts. chicken or beef stock
- 2 15-oz. cans sliced stewed tomatoes
- ¼ tsp. white pepper
- 1 tsp. fresh chopped cilantro
- 2 tbsp. hot sauce or 3–5 drops Tabasco sauce
- ½ tbsp. brown sugar
- ¼ tsp. salt
- ⅛ tsp. nutmeg
- Wide egg noodles, cooked according to package directions

SERVING THE NOODLES SEPARATELY FORMALIZES THE PRESENTATION AND THE SOUP, MINUS THE NOODLES, FREEZES EXTREMELY WELL.

DIRECTIONS

In a 6-quart stockpot, heat the olive oil and sauté the onions until just golden. Stir in the garlic, celery, potatoes, carrots and tomatoes. Cover, reduce heat to low and simmer 10 minutes. Stir in the stock, pepper, cilantro, hot sauce, sugar, salt and nutmeg. Adjust seasoning as desired.

Add the venison and bring to just a boil. Reduce heat and simmer covered for 30–45 minutes or until the potatoes and carrots are tender. Serve the soup in a tureen with the cooked noodles in a separate bowl. Allow your guests to individually portion the soup and noodles into large soup bowls. Garnish with cilantro leaves.

THAI VENISON SHANK SOUP

 SERVES 6–8

INGREDIENTS

- 8 pieces venison shank, cut 1½–2" thick
- 3 tbsp. vegetable oil
- 3 tbsp. minced garlic
- 4 bay leaves
- 1 tbsp. black peppercorns
- 1 tbsp. white peppercorns
- ¼ cup fish sauce
- ¼ cup oyster sauce
- ¼ cup teriyaki sauce
- ¼ cup rice wine vinegar
- 2 tbsp. sesame oil
- 2 tom yum soup cubes (available from your local oriental food store)
- 4 medium potatoes cut into 1" dice
- 4 medium carrots cut into ½" rounds
- 4 medium onions, sliced ½" thick and quartered
- 1 small head of cabbage, cored, quartered and sliced lengthwise

FOR ADDITIONAL "HEAT", ADD A THIRD SOUP CUBE AND A MINCED THAI CHILI PEPPER.

DIRECTIONS

Place the venison shank pieces in a large soup pot with water to cover. Add 2 bay leaves, bring to a boil. Reduce heat, cover and simmer 20 minutes. Drain the shank pieces and pat dry. Strain the cooking liquid and reserve for later use.

Heat an 8-quart stockpot over medium heat. Add the oil and brown the shank pieces on all sides. Add the garlic and onions, 2 bay leaves, peppercorns, fish sauce, teriyaki sauce and the soup cubes that have been dissolved in 1 quart of the reserved cooking liquid. Bring to a boil, reduce heat to low, cover and simmer 2 hours. Add additional cooking liquid as needed if the mixture becomes too thick.

Stir in the carrots and cook 20 minutes. Add the cabbage, potatoes and rice wine vinegar. Cover and simmer until potatoes and cabbage are tender, about 30 minutes. Adjust seasoning to taste—should be spicy and slightly salty.

Serve in large bowls over hot steamed rice.

GOULASH SOUP

SERVES 6–8

INGREDIENTS

- 2½ lbs. venison, cut into ¾" cubes
- 3 medium onions, cut in half and sliced
- 3–4 tbsp. Hungarian sweet or smoked paprika
- ¼ tsp. black pepper
- 6 medium potatoes, cut into 1" cubes
- 10 cups chicken stock
- 1 tsp. celery salt
- 2 bay leaves
- Olive oil

THIS SOUP CRIES OUT FOR A CAESAR SALAD AND A LOAF OF CRUSTY FRENCH BREAD.

DIRECTIONS

In a heavy skillet heat 2 tablespoons olive oil. Add onions and cook until slightly brown. Remove onions from skillet and drain on paper towel. Add 1 tablespoon olive oil to skillet and brown the venison in small batches, adding olive oil as necessary. Remove browned venison to a soup pot.

Add onions, paprika, pepper and celery to venison in soup pot. Cook on low heat, stirring to combine. Add the chicken stock and bay leaf. Cover and simmer for 20 minutes. Add the potatoes and continue simmering, covered, until the potatoes are tender, about 20 minutes. Adjust seasoning as desired.

HOT CHILI

SERVES 4–6

INGREDIENTS

- **1 lb. venison, cut into ½"–¾" cubes**
- **2 tbsp. olive oil**
- **2 cups chicken stock**
- **1 medium onion, peeled, sliced and chopped**
- **3–4 jalapeño peppers, seeded and cut into thin strips**
- **1 green bell pepper, seeded and chopped**
- **1 red bell pepper, seeded and chopped**
- **⅛ tsp. oregano**
- **1 tsp. minced garlic**
- **½ tsp. granulated garlic**
- **½ tsp. salt**
- **1 can tomato purée**
- **2 tsp. brown sugar**

DIRECTIONS

In a heavy dutch oven, heat the olive oil over medium-high heat. Add the venison and brown on all sides. Add all remaining ingredients and mix well. Reduce heat to medium and simmer, uncovered, for 30–40 minutes, stirring occasionally. Venison should be tender.

Serve in bowls garnished with shredded cheese, chopped green onion and/or sliced black olives.

THIS CHILI IS VERY SPICY. IF YOU WISH TO SOFTEN IT UP A BIT, ADD 2 CANS OF KIDNEY BEANS, ANOTHER CAN OF TOMATO PURÉE AND ANOTHER TBSP. OF BROWN SUGAR.

SPICY VENISON AND CORN CHOWDER

SERVES 8

INGREDIENTS

- 1½ lb. boneless venison, cut into 1" cubes
- Salt and pepper
- 3 tbsp. flour
- 3 tbsp. olive oil
- 2 cups chicken stock
- 2 cups frozen whole kernel corn, thawed
- 1½ cups tomato sauce
- 1 can diced tomatoes and green chilies
- 1 large onion, peeled, sliced and chopped
- 1 tsp. minced garlic
- 1½ tsp. ground cumin
- 1 tsp. chili powder
- 1½ tsp. smoked paprika
- ⅛ tsp. white pepper
- Pinch of crushed red pepper

THIS HEARTY CHOWDER IS BEST SERVED WITH CORN CHIPS AND GARNISHED WITH GREEN ONION AND SHREDDED CHEESE.

DIRECTIONS

Season the venison with salt and pepper. Place venison in a large plastic bag. Add the flour and shake until the venison is well coated.

Heat the oil in a medium dutch oven over medium heat. Brown the venison on all sides. Transfer the venison to a slow cooker. Add the remaining ingredients. Cover and cook on low 4–5 hours.

VENISON CHILI WITH CHORIZO SAUSAGE

SERVES 6–8

INGREDIENTS

- 2 lbs. ground venison
- 1 medium onion, peeled, sliced and quartered
- 2 tsp. minced garlic
- 1 lb. cooked chorizo sausage, cut in half lengthwise and sliced
- ¼ cup brown sugar
- 4 tbsp. chili powder
- 1 tsp. ground cumin
- 3 15-oz. cans stewed tomatoes
- 1 jar of your favorite spaghetti sauce

DIRECTIONS

In a 4-quart dutch oven, brown the venison in 1 tablespoon olive oil. Add the garlic and onion. Reduce heat and simmer until the onions are opaque. Add the remaining ingredients. Simmer for 1–1½ hours. Adjust seasoning to taste with salt and pepper.

LEFTOVER CHILI CAN BE USED FOR TOPPING
ON SAUSAGE SANDWICHES OR HOT DOGS.

VENISON CHILI WITH ITALIAN SAUSAGE

INGREDIENTS

- 2 lbs. venison roast cut into 1" cubes
- 1 lb. fresh spicy Italian sausage (bulk or casing removed)
- 2 tbsp. chopped garlic
- 2 serrano peppers, seeded and finely chopped
- 2 green bell peppers, seeded and finely chopped
- 2 medium onions, peeled, sliced and chopped
- 1 tsp. cumin
- 1 26-oz. can crushed tomatoes or tomato purée
- 1 15-oz. can diced tomatoes
- 2 15-oz. cans kidney beans

DIRECTIONS

In a heavy dutch oven or soup kettle, heat 2 tablespoons olive oil over medium heat and brown the venison in several batches. Brown the Italian sausage and then add the garlic, peppers, onion and cumin. Cook for 3–4 minutes. Add the venison, tomatoes and beans. Cover and simmer for 2 hours.

FOR A FESTIVE PRESENTATION, SERVE GARNISHED WITH SHREDDED CHEESE, SLICED GREEN ONION AND CHOPPED BLACK OLIVES.

STEWS & CASSEROLES

AUSSIE MARINATED VENISON

 SERVES 6–8

INGREDIENTS

- 3 lb. venison roast, cut into 1½" cubes
- 3 cups strong Australian beer
- 1½ tsp. salt
- ¼ tsp. white pepper
- 1 tbsp. minced garlic
- 1 medium onion, peeled and sliced
- 3 tbsp. butter
- 3 tbsp. olive oil
- ½ cup orange juice
- 1½ tbsp. cornstarch
- 1 tbsp. orange zest
- 1 tbsp. lemon zest
- 3 tbsp. currant jelly
- 2 cups peeled and sliced carrots
- ½ cup dried cranberries
- 1 small onion, peeled, sliced and chopped

THIS DISH CAN BE SERVED AS AN HOR D'OEUVRE FROM A CHAFING DISH—JUST CUT THE VENISON INTO SMALLER 1" CUBES.

DIRECTIONS

In a glass or stainless steel bowl, mix together the beer, salt, pepper, chopped medium onion and garlic. Add the venison. Cover and refrigerate for 24 hours.

Drain venison, reserving the beer marinade. Remove and discard the onions.

Heat a 3–4 quart dutch oven. Melt the butter and olive oil and brown the venison, in small batches, on all sides. Return all venison to the dutch oven. Add the carrots, small chopped onion, dried cranberries and the reserved marinade. Cover and braise over low heat for 2½ - 3 hours or until the venison is tender.

Mix the cornstarch with the orange juice and slowly stir into the braised venison. Add the jelly and citrus zests and continue cooking over low heat for 10 minutes. Adjust seasoning to taste. Serve over steamed rice.

SOUTHWESTERN CASSEROLE

SERVES 6–8

INGREDIENTS

- 2 lbs. ground venison
- 2 tbsp. olive oil
- 2 medium onions, peeled, sliced and chopped
- 6 stalks celery, sliced and chopped
- 2 packages taco seasoning
- 1 can condensed tomato soup
- 1 cup chicken stock
- 8 oz. cream cheese
- 6–8 medium potatoes, peeled and sliced
- 1½ cups shredded Monterey jack cheese

A HEARTY ONE-DISH MEAL THAT CAN BE PREPARED SEVERAL DAYS IN ADVANCE. LEFTOVER PORTIONS CAN BE EASILY REHEATED IN THE MICROWAVE.

DIRECTIONS

In a 2–3 quart dutch oven, heat the olive oil over medium-high heat. Add the venison and stir-fry until no longer pink. Stir in the onion and celery and continue to cook for 3–4 minutes. Stir in the taco seasoning, soup and chicken stock and heat until almost boiling. Cube the cream cheese and stir into the venison mixture until well mixed.

Spray a glass 9x12 baking dish. To build the casserole, alternate layers of potato and venison, starting with potatoes and ending with the venison mixture. Top with the shredded cheese. Bake on a sheet pan in a 325 degree oven 60–70 minutes or until casserole is set and bubbly. Let stand 15 minutes before serving.

CAMP STEW

INGREDIENTS

- 3 to 4 lbs. venison cut into 1½" cubes
- ¼ lb. butter
- ½ cup olive oil
- 3 tbsp. chopped garlic (12 cloves)
- ½ cup Worcestershire sauce
- 6 serrano peppers or 3 jalapeño peppers, seeded and chopped
- ½ tsp. white pepper

STOCK

- 3 cups beef broth
- 3 cups chicken stock
- 1 bottle red wine
- 4 carrots, peeled and sliced
- 1 16-oz. package frozen peas
- 1 10-oz. package frozen corn
- 2 onions, peeled, sliced and quartered
- 1 10-oz. package frozen green beans
- 1 lb. mushrooms, quartered
- 2 15-oz. cans sliced stewed tomatoes
- 8 medium red potatoes, quartered

ROUX

- 3 tbsp. butter
- 3 tbsp. flour

DIRECTIONS

In a large frypan or sauté pan, melt ⅓ of the butter and oil over medium-high heat. Add the venison in batches, browning on all sides. Add additional butter and oil as needed.

Move the browned meat to a large bowl. Mix together the garlic, Worcestershire sauce, peppers and white pepper. Stir this mixture into the meat.

In a large stockpot, combine the beef broth, chicken stock and red wine. Heat to almost a boil. Add the carrots, peas, corn, onion, green beans, mushrooms, stewed tomatoes and venison. Bring to a slow boil. Reduce heat, cover and simmer for 1½ hours. Add the potatoes and cook for an additional hour.

Prepare the roux by mixing together the melted butter and flour. Place 2 cups of liquid from the stew in a small pot. Slowly add the roux, whisking constantly. Return this mixture to the large pot and cook until the potatoes are tender and the stew has thickened.

FOR A ZESTIER FLAVOR, SUBSTITUTE 3 CANS
OF DARK BEER FOR THE RED WINE.

VENISON AND WILD RICE GUMBO

 SERVES 8

INGREDIENTS

- 2 lbs. venison roast, sliced and cut into 1" cubes
- 4 tbsp. olive oil
- 1 lb. bacon, cooked and crumbled
- 1 lb. smoked andouille or chorizo sausage, cut in half lengthwise and sliced ¼" thick
- 3 qts. chicken stock
- 2 packages frozen sliced okra
- 3 stalks celery, sliced
- 1 large onion, diced
- 1 tbsp. Cajun seasoning
- 1 seeded and minced jalapeño pepper
- 2 tsp. dried oregano
- 2 tsp. thyme
- 2 15-oz. cans sliced stewed tomatoes
- 1½ cups cooked wild rice
- ¼ cup balsamic vinegar (optional)

TO PREPARE A TRADITIONAL ROUX, MELT BUTTER AND WISK IN AN EQUAL AMOUNT OF FLOUR. COOK, WISKING CONSTANTLY, UNTIL THE ROUX IS NUTTY BROWN.

DIRECTIONS

Heat a heavy skillet over medium-high heat. In 4 batches, brown the venison in 1 tablespoon olive oil. Move venison to a 6-quart stockpot. Add the bacon, sausage, onion, celery, pepper and chicken stock. Bring to a boil over medium heat. Reduce heat to low and add the remaining herbs and spices, stewed tomatoes, and cooked wild rice. Cover and simmer 1 hour, stirring occasionally. Add the okra and balsamic vinegar. To thicken, gradually add 1 cup of hot stock to a roux prepared with 3 tablespoons flour and 3 tablespoons butter. Return this mixture to the gumbo and stir until thickened.

HUNTING CAMP ITALIAN CASSEROLE

SERVES 12

INGREDIENTS

- **3 lbs. ground venison**
- **4 tbsp. olive oil**
- **1 large onion, peeled, sliced and chopped**
- **2 jars marinara or spaghetti sauce**
- **½ lb. fresh mushrooms, sliced**
- **½ tsp. granulated garlic**
- **¼ tsp. crushed dried oregano**
- **2–3 tsps. brown sugar**
- **1 16-oz. package mostaciolli noodles, cooked and drained**
- **8 oz. sliced pepperoni or 8-oz. sliced chorizo sausage**
- **12 oz. provolone or mozzarella cheese, shredded**

I HAVE BEEN TOLD THIS

TASTES LIKE PIZZA

WITHOUT THE CRUST.

DIRECTIONS

In a large dutch oven, heat the oil and brown the venison in batches. Stir in the onion and mushrooms and cook over low heat for 3–4 minutes, stirring occasionally. Add the marinara sauce, garlic, oregano, brown sugar and mix thoroughly. Sauce should be thick but not pasty. If too thick, add 1 cup red wine. Continue cooking until heated through.

Ladle 3 cups sauce into a 4–5 quart slow cooker, top with ⅓ of the noodles, ⅓ of the sausage and ⅓ of the cheese. Repeat these layers. Cover and cook on medium-high for 2 hours or until cheese is melted.

MASHED POTATO, VENISON AND SPINACH PIE

 SERVES 6–8

INGREDIENTS

- 1½ lb. boneless venison loin cut into thin strips 1x2"
- 1 tsp. smoked paprika
- 1 tsp. crushed oregano
- ⅛ tsp. salt
- ⅛ tsp. white pepper
- 3 tbsp. unsalted butter
- 2 tbsp. olive oil
- 1 package frozen chopped spinach, thawed
- 2 large sweet onions, peeled, cut in half and thinly sliced
- 1 tsp. minced garlic
- 6–8 potatoes, cooked and mashed
- ⅓ cup heavy cream
- ⅓ cup chicken stock
- 1½ tbsp. malt vinegar
- ¼ tsp. salt
- ¼ tsp. white pepper
- Dash of nutmeg
- 1 cup grated sharp cheddar cheese
- 1 cup grated asiago cheese

FOR A TASTY VARIATION, USE VENISON SAUSAGE INSTEAD OF
VENISON LOIN AND OMIT THE PAPRIKA, OREGANO, SALT AND PEPPER.

DIRECTIONS

Preheat oven to 325 degrees. Butter or spray a 9x13" baking dish.

Drain excess moisture from the thawed spinach.

Using a large skillet, heat 1 tablespoon olive oil and 1 tablespoon butter. Sauté onion until just golden. Stir in the garlic and continue cooking for 1 minute. Transfer onion and garlic to a bowl. Season the venison with a mixture of the paprika, oregano, salt and pepper. Heat remaining butter and olive oil in the skillet. Add the venison and stir-fry until cooked and tender, 5–6 minutes. Toss the cooked venison and spinach in the bowl with the cooked onion and garlic.

In a large bowl, mix the mashed potatoes with the heavy cream, chicken stock, vinegar, salt and pepper, nutmeg and ½ cup of each of the cheeses.

Spread the potato mixture evenly in the bottom of the baking dish. Top with the venison and spinach mixture and then the remaining cheeses. Bake until the cheese is bubbling, 30–35 minutes. Cool slightly before serving.

MOROCCAN STEW

 SERVES 8

INGREDIENTS

- 3 lbs. boneless venison, cut into 1" cubes
- All-purpose flour
- 8 tbsp. butter
- ¼ tsp. ground cumin
- ½ tsp. cinnamon
- ¼ tsp. ground coriander
- ¼ tsp. cardamom
- 6 whole peppercorns
- 1 large onion, sliced and quartered
- 1 large green bell pepper, seeded and chopped
- 2 tsp. chopped garlic
- 3 cups chicken stock
- Dash cayenne pepper
- ¼ cup golden raisins
- ¼ cup dried cranberries
- ¼ cup slivered almonds
- Salt and pepper

REFRIGERATING FOR SEVERAL DAYS BEFORE SERVING ENHANCES THE FLAVORS OF THIS DISH.

DIRECTIONS

Dredge venison in flour, lightly coating. In a large skillet, melt 4 tablespoons butter over medium heat. Add the venison in batches. Brown on all sides. Remove venison from pan and set aside.

In a 5–6 quart dutch oven, heat 3 tablespoons butter over medium heat. Stir in the onion, green pepper and garlic. Reduce heat to low, cover and cook for 3–4 minutes. Stir spices into the onion mixture. Add the venison, raisins, dried cranberries and chicken stock. Stir together well and adjust flavor with salt, pepper and cayenne pepper.

Cover and simmer 45 minutes to 1 hour or until venison is tender. Serve over rice or couscous.

MOTHER MARY'S VENISON STEW

SERVES 8

INGREDIENTS

- 3 lbs. venison roast cut into 1" cubes
- 2 large onions sliced 1" thick and quartered
- 3 stalks celery, finely chopped
- 4 carrots, peeled and cut into bite-size pieces
- 2 large potatoes, peeled and cut into ¾" dice
- 1 package frozen baby peas
- 1 15-oz. can tomato sauce
- 1 tbsp. brown sugar
- ½ tsp. white pepper
- 1 tsp. chopped garlic
- 1 tsp. thyme
- 1 or 2 bay leaves
- 2 cups chicken stock

DIRECTIONS

In a heavy skillet or sauté pan, brown the venison in a small amount of olive oil over medium-high heat in several batches. As the venison browns, transfer it to a 4-quart oven-proof covered casserole.

In the heavy skillet or sauté pan, cook the onions, celery and carrots over medium low heat for 5–6 minutes. Add the cooked vegetables peas and potatoes to the venison in the casserole.

In a large bowl, mix together the remaining ingredients. Add to venison mixture in the casserole and stir well. Cover and bake in a preheated 325 degree oven for 2–3 hours or until the venison is fork-tender and the potatoes are cooked. Serve over buttered baked potatoes or pasta.

Pearl onions will formalize this dish. If you like, thicken the stew with 2 tablespoons cornstarch mixed in 1 cup water. On the stovetop, heat the cooked stew to almost boiling. Stir in the cornstarch mixture and continue stirring until the stew has thickened, approximately 3–5 minutes.

MUSTARD HERB VENISON

SERVES 6–8

INGREDIENTS

- 2 lbs. boneless venison, cut into 1x1½" strips
- ½ cup all-purpose flour
- 2 tbsp. olive oil
- 2 medium onions, peeled and cut into 8 wedges each
- 8 oz. fresh mushrooms, quartered
- 6 small Yukon gold potatoes, quartered
- 2 tbsp. spicy brown or Dijon mustard
- 2 cups beef stock
- 1 12-oz. bottle dark porter beer (substitute NA beer if desired)
- 3 medium carrots, peeled and cut into 1" thick pieces
- 1 16-oz. can tomato purée
- 1 tbsp. brown sugar
- 1 bay leaf
- 1 tsp. dried parsley
- ½ tsp. dried crushed thyme
- ½ tsp. black pepper
- ½ tsp. salt

VENISON CAN BE BROWNED, COOLED, PACKAGED IN PORTIONS AND FROZEN. THIS WILL JUMPSTART YOUR FAVORITE RECIPES.

DIRECTIONS

In a large bowl, combine the flour, salt, pepper, parsley, and thyme. Add the venison and toss until evenly coated. Reserve any remaining flour mixture.

In a 6-quart dutch oven, heat the oil over medium-high heat. Brown the venison on all sides. Add the onion, mushrooms, carrots and potatoes. Stir in any remaining flour mixture, the tomato purée and mustard. Cook 3–4 minutes. Add the beef stock, beer, and bay leaf. Bring to a boil. Reduce heat, cover and simmer 1½–2 hours or until venison is tender. Serve in bowls with your favorite bread.

TEXAS VENISON AND BEANS

 SERVES 6–8

INGREDIENTS

- 8 strips bacon, chopped
- 2 lbs. boneless venison, cut into 1" cubes
- 1 green bell pepper, seeded and diced
- 1 red bell pepper, seeded and diced
- 1 large onion, peeled and diced
- 1 16-oz. can tomato purée
- 2 tsp. minced garlic
- 2 tbsp. chili powder
- ½ tsp. ground cumin
- ½ tsp. crushed red pepper
- ½ lb. dried pinto beans
- ½ lb. cranberry beans
- 6 cups water

IN A HURRY? OMIT THE DRIED BEANS, COOK THE VENISON AND VEGETABLES FOR 4 HOURS. ADD 3 CANS OF YOUR FAVORITE BAKED BEANS AND COOK 1–2 HOURS MORE.

DIRECTIONS

Soak the beans in water 24 hours in the refrigerator.

Brown the bacon and place in the slow cooker. Drain and add the beans and stir in the spices. Add the venison, peppers, onion, garlic and tomatoes. Stir to distribute evenly. Cover and cook on low 8–10 hours.

SPANISH RAGOUT OF VENISON

SERVES 6–8

INGREDIENTS

- 3 lbs. venison, cut into 1" cubes
- 1 cup pitted prunes
- 1 cup dried apricots
- 1 cup sherry
- 1 cup pitted kalamata olives
- 1 jar roasted red peppers, drained and chopped
- ¼ cup red wine vinegar
- ¼ cup olive oil
- 1 small jar capers
- 3 tbsp. minced garlic
- 1 tbsp. dried oregano
- 1 tsp. hot chili powder
- 1 tbsp. smoked paprika
- 2 15-oz. cans stewed tomatoes, chopped
- 1 cup dry white wine
- ⅓ cup brown sugar
- 2 cups chicken stock

THIS RAGOUT HAS WONDERFUL FLAVORS AND CAN BE FROZEN FOR A SPECIAL MAKE-AHEAD MEAL.

DIRECTIONS

Thickener: Mix in a small bowl 1 tablespoon red wine vinegar, 3 tablespoons water and 2 tablespoons flour.

In a large stainless steel bowl, mix together the venison, olives, peppers, vinegar, oil, capers (including liquid), garlic, oregano, chili powder and paprika. Cover and refrigerate overnight.

Place the apricots and prunes in a glass or ceramic bowl with the sherry. Cover and refrigerate overnight.

Preheat oven to 325 degrees. In a 6–8 quart dutch oven, combine the venison and apricot/prune mixtures. Mix in the tomatoes, white wine, brown sugar and enough chicken stock to just cover the mixture. On the stovetop, bring the mixture to a boil. Cover and place in the oven. Bake for 1 hour. Remove the cover and continue baking for 35 minutes. Cool to room temperature and refrigerate overnight.

Remove any fat on the surface and reheat on the stovetop over medium heat, stirring occasionally, until the mixture comes to a boil. Stir in the thickener, reduce heat and simmer, stirring occasionally, until thickened.

VENISON BURGANDY

 SERVES 6–8

INGREDIENTS

- 4 slices bacon, chopped
- 2 tbsp. vegetable oil
- 2½ lb. venison, cut into 1" cubes
- ¼ cup flour
- 3 tbsp. vegetable oil
- ½ tsp. seasoned salt
- ¼ tsp. thyme
- 2 tsp. minced garlic
- 2 beef bouillon cubes dissolved in 1 cup hot water
- 1 cup burgundy wine (or any dry red wine)
- ½ lb. mushrooms, quartered
- 1 package frozen pearl onions
- 2 tbsp. cornstarch
- 3 tbsp. water

MASHED POTATOES
ARE A MUST SIDE DISH
ALONG WITH STEAMED
GREEN BEANS.

DIRECTIONS

In a large skillet or sauté pan, cook the bacon just to render the fat. Transfer bacon to a slow cooker. Dredge the venison in the flour and brown on all sides, adding vegetable oil as necessary. Work in small batches, transferring each to the slow cooker.

In a large bowl, stir together the seasoned salt, thyme, garlic, bouillon and wine. Add to the slow cooker. Cover and cook on low 6–8 hours or until the venison is tender. Mix the cornstarch and water and stir into the slow cooker. Increase heat to high and add the mushrooms and onions. Cook an additional 15 minutes.

VENISON STEW PARNASSUS

SERVES 6–8

INGREDIENTS
- **3 lbs. venison stew meat cut into 1½" cubes**

SPICE MIX
- **4 tsp. sea salt**
- **½ tsp. black pepper**
- **½ tsp. white pepper**
- **2 tsp. crushed dried oregano**
- **¼ tsp. nutmeg**
- **½ tsp. granulated garlic**
- **½ cup olive oil**
- **1 large onion, peeled, sliced and cut in half**
- **2 green bell peppers, seeded and sliced into narrow strips**
- **2 medium eggplant, peeled, sliced and cut into 6 wedges per slice**
- **2 cups chicken stock**
- **2 15-oz. cans stewed tomatoes, chopped**

SERVE WITH AN ONION
AND CUCUMBER SALAD
WITH FETA CHEESE.

DIRECTIONS
Season the venison with the spice mix. Heat the oil in a 3–4 quart dutch oven. Brown the venison in batches and transfer to a holding pan. Brown the onion in the dutch oven. Return the venison to the dutch oven, stir in the chicken stock and tomatoes. Cover and simmer over low heat for 2 hours.

Stir in the green peppers and eggplant. Cover and cook an additional 30 minutes. Adjust flavor with additional seasoning mix if required. Serve over steamed white rice.

VENISON STEW WITH SQUASH

 SERVES 6–8

INGREDIENTS

- 2 lb. venison roast cut into 1" cubes
- 3 stalks celery, sliced
- 2 cups butternut squash, peeled, seeded and cut into 1" cubes
- 4 carrots, peeled and sliced (1½ cups)
- 1 large onion, peeled, sliced and chopped
- 2 15-oz. cans stewed tomatoes, chopped
- 4 cups chicken stock
- ½ tsp. dried thyme
- ⅛ tsp. dried sage
- ½ tsp. white pepper
- ½ tsp. celery salt

COMFORT FOOD AT ITS BEST. SERVE OVER HOMEMADE BUTTERMILK BISCUITS.

ROUX

- 3 tbsp. flour
- 3 tbsp. butter

DIRECTIONS

In a 4–5 quart slow cooker, mix the venison and remaining ingredients except for the flour and butter. Cover and cook on low 5–6 hours.

To thicken, remove 2 cups hot liquid to a large bowl. Melt the butter and stir in flour. Slowly whisk the hot liquid into the butter and flour mixture, then return to the slow cooker. Increase heat to medium-high. Cover and cook 30 minutes, stirring occasionally until thickened.

VENISON STEW

INGREDIENTS

- 3 lbs. venison stew meat cut into 2" squares
- 1 large onion, sliced and quartered
- 3 cloves garlic, minced
- 3 stalks celery, sliced
- 1 tbsp. dried parsley
- 1 tsp. rosemary
- 2 bay leaves
- 3 whole cloves
- 8 whole peppercorns, crushed
- 1 cup red wine
- ½ lb. sweet butter
- 1 cup chicken stock
- 4 medium carrots, sliced ¼" thick
- 3 medium potatoes, peeled and diced ¾"
- 1 cup baby peas
- 2 15-oz. cans sliced stewed tomatoes
- salt & pepper to taste

SERVE IN HEATED BOWLS WITH THICK, CRUSTY BREAD.

DIRECTIONS

Season venison with salt and pepper, cover and refrigerate 2–3 hours. In a large heavy skillet, melt 2 tablespoons butter and sauté the onion and celery until soft. Place the onion and celery in a 4–6 quart stockpot.

Heat the skillet over medium-high heat and melt ½ stick butter. Brown the venison in 3 batches on all sides and transfer to the stockpot. Add the chicken stock, wine, garlic and spices to the venison. Bring to a boil, reduce heat and simmer for 1 hour or until the venison is tender. Add potatoes, peas, carrots, and stewed tomatoes and simmer approximately 1 hour (until potatoes and carrots are tender).

BERLINER VENISON AND SAUERKRAUT

 SERVES 6–8

INGREDIENTS

- 3 lbs. boneless venison, cut into 1" cubes
- 3 tbsp. vegetable oil
- 1 large onion, peeled, sliced and cut in half
- ½ tsp. salt
- ½ tsp. black pepper
- 1 tsp. paprika
- 2 cups beef or chicken stock
- 2 lbs. sauerkraut, rinsed and drained
- 2 bay leaves
- 2 15-oz. cans stewed tomatoes, chopped

THE FLAVORS OF THIS DISH IMPROVE OVER TIME. I RECOMMEND PREPARING IT 1 TO 2 DAYS IN ADVANCE OF SERVING.

DIRECTIONS

Preheat oven to 325 degrees.

In a 3–4 quart dutch oven, heat the oil and brown the venison on all sides. Stir in the onion, salt, pepper, paprika and 1 cup stock. Cover and reduce heat to low and cook for 30 minutes, stirring often. Add remaining stock, bay leaves, sauerkraut and tomatoes. Mix well. Cover and bake for 2–2½ hours or until venison is tender.

BASQUE STEW

SERVES 6–8

INGREDIENTS

- 2 lbs. venison, cut into 1" cubes
- 1 lb. mild chorizo sausage, sliced into ¼ inch thick rounds
- 1 tsp. granulated garlic
- ⅓ cup fresh chopped parsley
- 1 butternut squash, peeled, seeded and cut into 1" cubes
- 3 carrots, peeled and diced
- 2 medium potatoes, cut into 1" cubes
- 1 large onion, peeled, thickly sliced and chopped
- 1 large green pepper, seeded, sliced and chopped
- 1 cup red wine
- ¼ cup peanut oil
- 2 15-oz. cans stewed tomatoes, chopped
- 3 tbsp. smoked paprika
- Salt and pepper

CHORIZO SAUSAGE IS THE PRIMARY FLAVOR ENHANCER IN THE RECIPE. THERE ARE NUMEROUS VARIETIES, RANGING FROM VERY MILD TO EXTREMELY SPICY. TRY SEVERAL DIFFERENT TYPES TO SELECT THE FLAVOR PROFILE YOU PREFER.

DIRECTIONS

Heat a 6-quart dutch oven over medium heat. Add the peanut oil and venison, cooking until browned. Add the chorizo sausage and cook 2–3 minutes. Stir in the paprika and garlic, followed by the parsley, squash, carrots, potatoes, onion and green pepper. Stir well. Add the tomatoes and red wine. Adjust seasoning to your taste with the salt and pepper.

Cover and reduce heat to low. Simmer 1–1½ hours or until the venison is tender and the vegetables are cooked.

STEAKS, ROASTS & CHOPS

BAYOU VENISON

SERVES 8

INGREDIENTS

- 2 lbs. boneless venison roast
- 2 cups. chopped onion
- 1 cup celery, sliced
- 2 cups seasoned tomato juice
- 1 tbsp. Worcestershire sauce
- ⅛ tsp. granulated garlic
- 1 green bell pepper, seeded and chopped
- 1 package frozen okra, thawed
- 1 can button mushrooms
- 1 tbsp. brown sugar (optional)
- Salt and pepper to taste

KICK THIS UP A NOTCH
WITH 1/2 OF A MINCED
JALAPEÑO PEPPER ADDED
DURING THE LAST 30
MINUTES OF COOKING.

DIRECTIONS

Slice venison ½" thick, then into 2–3" strips. Dust with salt, pepper and granulated garlic. Place the venison in a slow cooker with the onion, celery, tomato juice, Worcestershire sauce, and brown sugar. Cover and cook on low 5–6 hours. Add the green pepper, okra and mushrooms. Cover, increase heat to high for 20–30 minutes or until okra is tender. Serve over steamed rice.

BREADED VENISON CHOPS

 SERVES 4

INGREDIENTS
- 8 venison chops (allow at least 2 chops per person)
- 2 large eggs
- 3 tbsp. milk
- ½ cup vegetable oil

BREADING MIX
- 1 cup breadcrumbs
- ¼ cup grated Parmesan cheese
- 2 tsp. Italian seasoning, crushed
- ½ tsp. granulated garlic (optional)

THIS BREADING MIXTURE ALSO WORKS VERY WELL WITH PORK AND CHICKEN.

DIRECTIONS
Combine all breading mix ingredients. Place breading mix on a cookie sheet. In a medium bowl, whisk together the eggs and milk. Dip chops in the egg mixture and allow excess to drip off. Place the chops in the breading mix and coat both sides.

Heat a large skillet over medium-high heat. Add vegetable oil. Carefully place chops in the hot oil and turn after 1½–2 minutes. Chops should be nicely browned. Remove chops to baking pan. Place in a preheated 300 degree oven for 10–15 minutes. Serve with steamed vegetables and mashed potatoes.

BBQ VENISON CHOPS WITH WILD RICE PANCAKES

SERVES 8

BBQ SAUCE
- 1 cup teriyaki sauce
- ¼ cup cranberry juice
- ¼ cup brown sugar
- ¼ cup orange juice
- 2 cloves garlic, minced
- 1 small onion, peeled, sliced and minced
- ½ tsp. ground cumin
- 1 tbsp. butter

BBQ SAUCE DIRECTIONS
In a 1-quart saucepan, heat the butter and sauté the onion until opaque. Add the garlic and continue to cook 1 minute. Stir in the teriyaki sauce, juice, sugar and cumin. Reduce heat to low and simmer 5 minutes. Remove from heat and allow to cool 3–4 hours to fully develop the flavor.

WILD RICE PANCAKES
- 2 cups cooked wild rice
- ¼ cup finely chopped green onion
- ¼ tsp. granulated garlic
- 1 cup all-purpose flour
- ½ cup heavy cream
- 2 eggs, beaten
- ⅛ tsp. salt
- ⅛ tsp. white pepper
- 2 tbsp. olive oil
- 2 tbsp. butter

WILD RICE PANCAKE DIRECTIONS

In a large bowl, combine the wild rice, green onion, garlic, salt and pepper. In a stainless steel bowl, mix together the eggs and cream and slowly whisk in the flour. Combine this mixture with the wild rice and mix thoroughly. In a large skillet or sauté pan, heat the butter and oil. Add spoons of the batter to form a 6" pancake. Cook 2–3 minutes or until browned. Turn and brown the other side. Repeat to make 8 pancakes. Keep warm in a 200 degree oven.

CHOPS

- 8 venison loin chops cut 1" thick

CHOP DIRECTIONS

Preheat your grill to medium-high. Grill the chops 3–4 minutes (for rare to medium rare) on each side, basting with the BBQ sauce. Serve each chop on a pancake with extra sauce on the side.

THE WILD RICE PANCAKES ALSO MAKE A WONDERFUL BREAKFAST DISH—JUST OMIT THE ONION AND GARLIC AND SERVE WITH MAPLE SYRUP OR HOMEMADE PRESERVES.

CAROLINA BBQ

INGREDIENTS

- 4–5 lb. venison shoulder roast
- 1 large onion, peeled, sliced and chopped
- 4 stalks celery, sliced
- 2 carrots, peeled and sliced
- 8 peppercorns
- 2 cups red wine
- 2 cups chicken stock
- 2 bay leaves

TRADITIONALLY, THESE SANDWICHES ARE SERVED TOPPED WITH COLESLAW.

BBQ SAUCE

- 1 medium onion, peeled, sliced and chopped
- 1 tsp. minced garlic
- 2 tbsp. butter
- 2 cups prepared yellow mustard
- 1½ cup brown sugar
- 1½ cup cider vinegar
- 4 tbsp. chili powder
- 2 tsp. black pepper
- 2 tsp. white pepper
- ½ tsp. cayenne pepper
- 1 cup teriyaki sauce

DIRECTIONS

Place the venison and vegetables in a large slow cooker. Add peppercorns, bay leaves, wine, chicken stock and water to cover. Cook on low heat 6–8 hours or until venison is very tender. Remove venison to a tray and allow to cool until it can be shredded by hand. Place in a large bowl. If you'd like, save the stock for later use in soups or sauces.

Keep the shredded pork warm if you plan to serve it immediately or cool in the refrigerator for later use.

To prepare the BBQ sauce, melt the butter over medium heat in a 3–4 quart dutch oven. Sauté the onion until opaque. Stir in the garlic and cook 1–2 minutes. Reduce the heat to low and stir in the remaining sauce ingredients. Cook 5 minutes, stirring often. Remove sauce from the heat. Add 2 cups to the venison and mix well. Serve on fresh Kaiser rolls with additional sauce on the side.

CHICKEN FRIED VENISON STEAK

SERVES 6–8

INGREDIENTS

- 2–3 lbs. boneless venison steak, ½" thick
- 1½ tbsp. sea salt or kosher salt
- 1 tbsp. white vinegar
- ¼ cup white wine
- 2–3 cups water
- 2½ cups all-purpose flour
- 2 tsp. black pepper
- 2 tsp. white pepper
- ½ tsp. granulated garlic
- ⅛ tsp. nutmeg
- ½ tsp. paprika
- ¼–½ cup olive oil

ADD 1 CUP EACH OF BABY
PEAS AND PEARL ONIONS
TO THE GRAVY FOR ADDED
FLAVOR AND COLOR.

CREAM GRAVY

- 2 tbsp. all-purpose flour
- 2 tbsp. butter
- 1 chicken bouillon cube, crushed and mixed with ½ cup hot water
- 2 cups heavy cream

DIRECTIONS

Tenderize the venison with a meat mallet. Cut each slice in half crosswise. Place venison in a large stainless steel or glass bowl. Mix the salt, vinegar and wine with the water and pour over the venison. Add additional water to completely cover the venison. Cover the bowl with plastic wrap and refrigerate at least 3 hours.

In a large plastic bag, combine the flour, pepper, garlic, nutmeg and paprika. Remove the venison from the marinade and towel off excess liquid. Add the venison to the flour and spice mixture in the plastic bag, 2 pieces at a time, shake to coat and remove to a large holding tray.

In a large deep skillet or sauté pan, heat the olive oil over medium-high heat. Carefully add the venison steaks in small batches and fry until light brown, 30–60 seconds per side. Drain on paper towels and transfer to a warm baking pan. Place pan in a 300 degree oven.

To make the gravy, melt the butter in a 1 quart saucepan. Whisk in the flour and bouillon. Stir until combined and smooth. Slowly whisk in the heavy cream, reduce heat to low and stir until thickened.

Arrange venison on a warm platter and spoon the gravy over the steaks.

STEAK AU POIVRE

 SERVES 6

INGREDIENTS

- 3 lbs. venison, short loin or strip loin, cut into 8 oz. steaks at least 1" thick and tenderized with a spring loaded multi-blade meat tenderizer or textured meat mallet
- 4 tbsp. white and black peppercorns, coarsely ground or crushed Dijon mustard
- 1 tbsp. olive oil

DIJON CREAM SAUCE

- ½ cup minced shallots
- 1 clove garlic, minced
- 1 cup beef stock, mixed with 1 tbsp. Knorr Demi-Glace Sauce Mix
- 2 tbsp. butter
- 1 tbsp. Dijon mustard
- ¼ cup brandy

THE DIJON CREAM SAUCE WILL ENHANCE ANY WILD OR DOMESTIC RED OR WHITE MEAT. FOR AN ADDED PUNCH, USE COGNAC INSTEAD OF BRANDY.

DIRECTIONS

Spread a thin layer of Dijon mustard on each side of the steak, press into the peppercorns to coat.

Heat a heavy, seasoned skillet to a level where a drop of water bounces on the surface. Add the olive oil and brown the steaks 2 minutes on each side. Reduce heat and cook to desired degree of doneness.

Melt the butter in a 2-quart saucepan and gently sauté the shallot and garlic over low heat until translucent. Whisk in the mustard, beef stock and brandy. Continue stirring until the sauce has thickened.

To serve, plate the steaks and spoon the sauce over.

LEMON VENISON CHOPS

 SERVES 6–8

INGREDIENTS

- 6–8 bone-in venison chops, cut 1" thick
- ½ tsp. seasoned salt
- ¼ tsp. white pepper
- 1 large onion, peeled and sliced
- 2 lemons, sliced ¼" thick
- ⅓ cup light brown sugar
- ⅓ cup ketchup
- ⅓ cup red wine

WE ENJOY THIS DISH
WITH BABY PEAS AND
STEAMED RICE OR
BUTTERED EGG NOODLES.

DIRECTIONS

Season chops with salt and pepper. Place chops in a slow cooker, layer onion and lemon slices on top. In a bowl, mix together the brown sugar, ketchup, and wine. Pour over the chops in the slow cooker. Cover and cook on low for 6 hours or until tender.

POT-AU-FEU FOR TWO

 SERVES 2

INGREDIENTS

- 8–10 oz. venison tenderloin, trimmed of all fat, gristle and silver skin
- 2 boneless chicken thighs
- 6 strips bacon, chopped
- ¼ cup minced onion
- 1 clove garlic, crushed and minced
- 2 cups chicken stock
- 1 cup white wine
- ¼ cup teriyaki sauce
- 6 baby carrots, scraped and trimmed
- 1 turnip, peeled and cut in 1" dice
- 1 leek, white part only, cut in half in 2" sections and washed
- 20 tiny French green beans (haricot vert)
- 6 fresh shitake mushrooms, stem removed
- 10 peppercorns
- 1 bay leaf
- 6 coriander leaves

THE NATURAL PARTNER TO THIS DISH IS THIS TOMATO SAUCE.

TOMATO SAUCE

- 1 tbsp. each of butter and olive oil
- ½ cup chopped onion
- 1 15-oz. can sliced stewed tomatoes, chopped
- Salt and pepper to taste
- 2 tbsp. freshly grated or prepared horseradish (excess moisture removed)
- ½ cup heavy cream

DIRECTIONS

In a 1-quart saucepan, heat the butter and olive oil. Add the onion and garlic and cook until opaque. Add the tomatoes, salt and pepper and bring to a boil. Reduce heat and simmer 5 minutes. Stir in the horseradish and cream. Now all you need is a crisp green salad and a loaf of garlic bread to finish this dish off.

Using a 4-quart dutch oven, cook the bacon until rendered of all fat. Remove and reserve the bacon. Add the chicken thighs, skin side down, season with salt and pepper and cook 2–3 minutes. Add the reserved bacon, onion and garlic and cook for 2–3 minutes longer.

Stir in the chicken stock, wine, teriyaki sauce, peppercorns and bay leaf. Bring to almost a boil and add the leeks, carrots and turnips. Cover and simmer 15–20 minutes or until the chicken is cooked and the vegetables are tender crisp. Add the venison, mushrooms and green beans. Cover and continue cooking until the venison is set (springs back from the touch).

Remove the venison and slice into 2 portions. In 2 heated soup plates or pasta dishes, divide the chicken and vegetables and arrange artistically. Top with venison slices and hot broth. Garnish with coriander leaves and tomato sauce on the side.

RHEINISCHER STUFFED VENISON ROAST

SERVES 6–8

INGREDIENTS

- 4 lb. venison roast, butterflied
- 1 tsp. salt
- ¼ tsp. black pepper
- ¼ tsp. paprika
- 6 tbsp. butter
- 1 medium onion, peeled, sliced and chopped
- 4 oz. fresh mushrooms, chopped
- 2 cups seasoned breadcrumbs
- ⅓ cup sour cream

- 2 eggs, beaten
- ⅛ tsp. nutmeg
- 1 tbsp. parsley, minced
- 1 cup red wine
- 1 cup water
- 2 tbsp. red wine vinegar
- 3 carrots, peeled and sliced
- 1 large onion, peeled, sliced and quartered
- 1 bay leaf

DIRECTIONS

Season the venison with salt, pepper and paprika. In a large sauté pan, melt 4 tablespoons butter and stir in the onions. Cook for 3–4 minutes. Stir in the mushrooms and sauté for 5 minutes. Mix in the breadcrumbs, sour cream, eggs, and nutmeg. Spread the stuffing over the venison, roll up and tie with kitchen twine.

In a dutch oven, melt 2 tablespoons butter and brown the venison on all sides. Add the wine, water, vinegar, carrot, onion and bay leaf. Cover and cook over low heat for 2½–3 hours or until the venison is tender. Turn and baste the roast several times while cooking.

Transfer venison to a hot platter. Let stand 10 minutes and remove the twine. Strain the pan juices and pour over the roast after slicing. Sprinkle with parsley. Serve any additional sauce at the table.

FOR A MORE ROBUST GRAVY, PURÉE THE CARROTS
AND ONIONS WITH THE PAN JUICES.

WARSAW VENISON

INGREDIENTS

- 4 lb. boneless venison roast
- 10 juniper berries, crushed
- Brine
- 1 cup red wine vinegar
- 3 cups water
- 8 black peppercorns
- 8 white peppercorns
- 2 bay leaves
- 1 large onion, peeled and sliced
- 3 tbsp. butter
- 2 tsp. salt
- 1 cup sour cream
- 1¼ cup finely chopped chives
- 1 clove garlic, crushed and minced

JUNIPER BERRIES ARE AN ACQUIRED TASTE AND ARE OFTEN DIFFICULT TO FIND—THEY ARE DEFINITELY AN OPTIONAL INGREDIENT IN THIS RECIPE.

DIRECTIONS

Rub the venison with the juniper berries and place in a glass bowl. In a 3-quart saucepan, combine the brine ingredients and bring to a boil over low heat. Turn off heat, cover and let stand 10–15 minutes. Pour the brine over the venison, using a weight to keep the roast submerged. Cover and refrigerate for 48 hours.

Drain the venison roast, reserving 2 cups of the brine liquid. Dry the roast, rub with salt and place on a rack in a shallow roasting pan. Roast in a 400 degree oven for 30 minutes. Reduce heat to 325 degrees and roast for 1½-2 hours.

Melt the butter in a small saucepan. Add the reserved brine liquid and heat through. Use this mixture to baste the roast every 15–20 minutes.

Remove roast from oven and let sit 15 minutes before carving.

Whisk together the sour cream, chives and garlic. Spoon sauce over the roast and serve on the side at the table.

ROAST VENISON WITH APRICOTS, PRUNES AND PEARS

 SERVES 8

INGREDIENTS
- 3–4 lb. boneless venison roast
- 16 dried apricots and 16 prunes, rehydrated in 2 cups cream sherry (allow at least 2 days)
- 6 strips bacon
- 4 ripe pears, cored and cut in half

SPICE RUB
- ¼ cup smoked paprika
- 1 tsp. granulated garlic
- ½ tsp. white pepper
- 1 package onion soup mix
- Mix together all spice rub ingredients in a small bowl.

BASTING SAUCE
- ¼ lb. butter
- 2 tbsp. minced garlic
- ½ cup honey
- ½ cup teriyaki sauce
- 2 cups white zinfandel wine
- 2 cups cranberry juice
- ½ tbsp. crushed dried tarragon

ADD A TEASPOON OF HOT SAUCE OR A FEW DROPS OF TABASCO TO SPARK UP THE SAUCE.

DIRECTIONS

Melt butter in a large saucepan over medium heat. Add the garlic, tarragon, honey and teriyaki sauce. Bring to a boil and stir in the wine and cranberry juice. Reduce heat to low and simmer 5 minutes. Allow to cool.

Preheat oven to 325 degrees.

Butterfly cut the roast. Lay cut side up and line the inside with bacon strips. Arrange the apricots and prunes in the center and fold over the sides to create a cylinder. Secure with kitchen twine. Dust the outside of the roast with the spice rub.

Place 5 whole carrots in the bottom of a large dutch oven and set the venison roast on the "carrot rack."

In a large skillet, heat 2 tablespoons vegetable oil over medium-high heat. Place the pears, cut side down, in the skillet and cook for 5–6 minutes. Place the pears around the venison in the dutch oven. Brush the roast and the pears with the basting sauce. Place the dutch oven in the oven, covered, and bake 50–60 minutes until the internal temperature of the roast reaches 145 degrees. Baste twice during baking.

Transfer the roast to a holding tray and let stand 10–15 minutes. Slice the venison 1" thick and place the slices on a warm platter, arrange the pears around the roast. Drizzle warm basting sauce over the roast and serve more at the table.

SAUERBRATEN

SERVES 6–8

INGREDIENTS
- **3–4 lb. venison roast**

MARINADE
- 1 cup dry red wine
- 1 cup red wine vinegar
- 2 cups cranberry juice
- 1 spice bag with 1 tbsp. pickling spice,
  2 bay leaves, 6 whole cloves and 10 peppercorns
- 1 medium onion, peeled and sliced

BRAISING LIQUID
- ¼ lb. butter
- ¼ lb. chopped bacon
- 1 cup chopped onion
- 1 cup chopped celery
- 1 cup chopped carrot
- 10 peppercorns, crushed
- 1 cup dry red wine
- ½ cup red wine vinegar
- 2 cups beef or chicken stock

SAUCE FINISH
- ½ cup Knorr Demi-Glace Sauce Mix
- 1 cup braising liquid
- 1 cup finely chopped ginger snap cookies (10–12 cookies)
- 1 cup cream sherry

THIS RECIPE SHOULD BE STARTED 3–4 DAYS BEFORE YOU PLAN TO SERVE IT. SWEET/SOUR CABBAGE AND MASHED POTATOES ARE THE IDEAL ACCOMPANIMENT.

DIRECTIONS

To make the marinade, bring cranberry juice to a boil in a 1-quart saucepan. Add spice bag, remove from the heat and allow to cool. Place venison roast in a 2½ gallon Ziploc bag. Add onions, cooled cranberry juice with the spice bag, red wine and red wine vinegar. Place bag in large bowl or deep pan and refrigerate for at least 2–3 days. Rotate and flip the bag 3 times each day.

Preheat oven to 325 degrees.

Remove the roast from the marinade. Wipe off excess moisture and place on a holding tray. Strain marinade, discarding the vegetables and spice bag, reserving the liquid. In a large, deep dutch oven, melt the butter and brown the roast on all sides. Remove the venison to a holding tray. Add the bacon to the dutch oven, stir and cook 3–4 minutes. Remove and reserve the bacon for the sauce. Add the celery, carrot and onion to the dutch oven, stirring and cooking for 5 minutes. Return the venison to the dutch oven. Add the peppercorns, wine, red wine vinegar and stock. Bring to a boil, cover and place in the oven for 2–3 hours or until venison is fork tender. Remove from the oven, uncover and cool to room temperature. Strain and discard the vegetables. Reserve the strained braising liquid. Refrigerate the venison and liquid overnight.

Remove excess fat from the surface of the braising liquid. Remove venison and slice ¼" thick and arrange in a decorative baking/serving dish. Heat 1 cup of the braising liquid over medium heat. Whisk in the sauce mix, gingersnaps, and sherry, whisking until the sauce thickens. Spoon sauce over the venison and warm in a 150 degree oven for 15–20 minutes.

VENISON SCHNITZEL

INGREDIENTS
- Boneless venison loin or leg slices, ¼" to ½" thick
- Cracker or seasoned breadcrumbs
- 1 beaten egg
- Unsalted butter

DIRECTIONS
Flatten the venison slices between 2 sheets of waxed paper. Dip the flattened slices in the beaten egg and then the crumbs, generously coating both sides.

Heat a large heavy skillet over medium-high heat. Melt 2 ounces butter. Quickly brown the venison on both sides. Drain on a paper towel and keep warm in a 200 degree oven. Serve with sweet and sour red cabbage and spatzle or boiled potatoes.

IF COOKING FOR A CROWD, TRANSFER THE SCHNITZEL
TO AN OVENPROOF TRAY LINED WITH PAPER TOWEL.
KEEP WARM IN A 200 DEGREE OVEN.

SOUTH OF THE BORDER VENISON

INGREDIENTS

- **2 lb. boneless venison roast**
- **2 cups cranberry juice**
- **1 tbsp. minced garlic**
- **¼ tsp. white pepper**
- **¼ tsp. salt**
- **1 tbsp. chili powder**
- **¼ tsp. ground cumin**
- **1 tbsp. Dijon mustard**
- **1 large onion, peeled and chopped**
- **1 tsp. beef base or 1 bouillon cube**
- **1 15-oz. can sliced stewed tomatoes, chopped**
- **1 16-oz. can kidney beans**

DRESS THIS DISH UP
BY TOPPING IT WITH
SHREDDED CHEESE AND
SLICED GREEN ONION.

DIRECTIONS

Slice the venison ½" thick then cut into strips about 1" wide. Dust the venison with salt, pepper, chili powder and cumin. Place venison, onion and tomatoes in a large bowl.

Mix the beef base with the mustard. Slowly whisk in the cranberry juice and garlic and add to the venison. Cover and cook on low for at least 6 hours. Add the beans and cook, covered, for 30 minutes. Serve over steamed rice.

CORIANDER AND HONEY GLAZED VENISON CHOPS

INGREDIENTS
- 6–8 boneless venison chops, cut 1½" thick
- 2 tbsp. olive oil
- 1 tbsp. ground coriander
- 2 tbsp. Dijon mustard
- ½ tsp. smoked paprika
- 3 tbsp. honey
- 2 tbsp. lime juice
- ¼ cup teriyaki

DIRECTIONS
Preheat oven to 400 degrees.

In a small bowl, mix together the coriander, mustard, paprika, honey, lime juice and teriyaki sauce.

In an ovenproof frying pan, heat the oil and sear the chops for 1½–2 minutes on each side. Apply coriander and honey glaze to both sides of the chops and place pan in the preheated oven for 8–10 minutes (chops will be rare to medium rare).

THE CORIANDER HONEY GLAZE CAN BE USED
ON STEAMED CARROTS OR WINTER SQUASH.

SZECHUAN VENISON WITH DRIED CRANBERRIES IN PORT WINE

 SERVES 2

INGREDIENTS

- 1 tbsp. Szechuan peppercorns
- 1 tbsp. black peppercorns
- 1 tbsp. white peppercorns
- 2 6-oz. venison tenderloin steaks
- 1 tbsp. olive oil
- ¼ cup dried cranberries, chopped in a food processor with ¼ tsp. dry mustard, then soaked in 1 cup ruby port wine
- ½ tsp. fresh grated ginger
- ¼ cup heavy cream
- 1 tbsp. chicken stock paste
- 1 tbsp. butter

FREEZE ANY REMAINING SAUCE IN ICE CUBE TRAYS AND STORE IN PLASTIC BAGS IN THE FREEZER.

DIRECTIONS

Chop peppers in a food processor or spice grinder. Rub pepper mixture over all sides of the tenderloin steaks.

In a heavy, seasoned skillet, heat the oil over high heat. Season the tenderloins with salt to taste and carefully place in the hot skillet. Cook 3 minutes per side for medium rare. Transfer tenderloins to a plate and cover with foil. Add the port wine and cranberries to the skillet. Stir in the chicken stock paste. Add the ginger. Bring to a boil and stir in the cream. Remove from the heat and wisk in the butter.

Plate the steaks and spoon sauce around.

THAI CURRY

INGREDIENTS

- 2 lbs. boneless venison cut into thin strips ½ x 2"
- 1–2 Thai chili peppers, minced
- 1 green bell pepper, seeded and cut into strips
- 1 red bell pepper, seeded and cut into strips
- 2 medium onions, peeled, cut in half and sliced

CURRY MIXTURE

- 1 15-oz. can unsweetened coconut milk
- 1 tbsp. red curry paste
- 1 tbsp. peanut butter
- 1 tbsp. brown sugar
- 1 tbsp. fish sauce
- 1 tbsp. oyster sauce
- 1 tbsp. lime juice
- ½ cup chicken stock
- 5–6 fresh basil leaves, thinly sliced

> THINLY SLICING THE MEAT WILL BE MUCH EASIER IF THE MEAT IS PARTIALLY FROZEN.

DIRECTIONS

In a wok, heat 1 tablespoon oil and stir-fry the venison for 2–3 minutes. Add the peppers and onion and continue cooking for 3 minutes.

In a large stainless steel bowl, whisk together the curry paste, peanut butter, brown sugar, fish sauce, oyster sauce, lime juice, chicken stock and coconut milk. Slowly add the curry mixture to the wok, cover and simmer for 2 minutes until the venison is tender and the sauce has thickened. Serve over steamed rice garnished with the fresh basil.

TERIYAKI VENISON

INGREDIENTS

- 6 venison steaks, cut into ¾" cubes
- 1 tbsp. canola oil
- 3 medium garlic cloves, minced
- ½ tsp. grated fresh ginger
- 6 oz. sugar snap peas
- 6 green onions, sliced
- 1 medium carrot, sliced into matchsticks
- 1 medium red bell pepper, cut into 1" dice

THIS TERIYAKI GLAZE WORKS EQUALLY WELL WITH CHICKEN.

TERIYAKI GLAZE

Whisk together, in a small bowl:

- ¼ cup cranberry juice,
- 3 tbsp. teriyaki sauce,
- ½ tsp. cornstarch
- 1 tsp. toasted sesame oil

DIRECTIONS

Heat a wok or large nonstick skillet over medium-high heat. Add oil, garlic, venison and ginger. Stir-fry until the venison is browned, about 3–4 minutes. Stir in the peas, carrot, green onion and red pepper and cook an additional 2–3 minutes. Add the teriyaki glaze and stir over low heat until thickened.

Serve over steamed rice or oriental noodles.

VENISON CHOPS AND SAUSAGE
WITH SAUERKRAUT

 SERVES 4–6

INGREDIENTS

- 6 venison loin chops, cut 1" thick and seasoned with salt and pepper
- 6 fresh Italian sausages, about 4 oz. each
- 4 tbsp. olive oil
- 1 medium onion, peeled, sliced and chopped
- 1 teaspoon minced garlic (about 2 cloves)
- 2 cups Riesling wine
- 1 bay leaf
- 2 cups chicken stock
- ¼ cup dried cranberries
- 1 large green apple, peeled, cored and chopped
- ½ tsp. marjoram
- ¼ tsp. caraway seeds (optional)

IF USING THE OPTIONAL CARAWAY SEED, MIX IT WITH THE SAUERKRAUT BEFORE ADDING TO THE COOKING POT.

DIRECTIONS

Heat 2 tablespoons olive oil in a large dutch oven. Brown the venison and sausage in small batches adding oil as needed. Remove meat to a holding tray.

Add the onion and garlic to the dutch oven. Cook and stir for 3–4 minutes. Add the apples, bay leaf, marjoram, dried cranberries, sauerkraut and mix thoroughly. Cook for 5–10 minutes. Remove ½ of the sauerkraut mixture to a stainless steel or glass bowl. Add the venison and sausage in layers with the reserved sauerkraut. Mix the wine and chicken stock and add to the ingredients in the dutch oven. Reduce heat to low, cover and simmer 45 minutes.

VENISON SHOULDER ROAST WITH APPLES, TURNIPS AND CARROTS

 SERVES 4–6

INGREDIENTS

- 3–4 lb. boned, rolled and tied venison shoulder roast
- 3 tbsp. butter
- 3 tbsp. olive oil
- 2 cups chicken stock
- 2 cups Riesling wine
- 1 medium onion, sliced and chopped
- 2 tsp. minced garlic
- 1 cup dried apples, reconstituted with 1 cup Riesling
- 12 baby carrots, peeled and trimmed
- 5 medium turnips, peeled and diced

ADD 1/4 CUP DRIED CRANBERRIES TO THE APPLES AND 1/2 CUP CRANBERRY JUICE TO THE RIESLING WINE FOR AN INTERESTING FLAVOR TWIST.

DIRECTIONS

In a 4–6 quart dutch oven, heat 2 tablespoons butter and 2 tablespoons olive oil and brown the roast on all sides. Remove the venison to a holding tray. Add remaining butter and olive oil to the dutch oven and sauté onion until golden. Reduce the heat and stir in the garlic, cooking 2 minutes. Add the roast, chicken stock, and wine. Cover and simmer over low heat 2–3 hours or until the venison is tender. Add the apples, carrots and turnips. Cover and cook another 20–30 minutes or until the vegetables are tender.

Slice roast and serve on a warmed platter surrounded by the vegetables and apples.

VENISON PICCATA

INGREDIENTS

- 8 pieces boneless venison, sliced ¼" thick and pounded thin between sheets of waxed paper
- 1 cup cracker crumbs
- 1 egg beaten with 1 tbsp. water
- ¼ lb. unsalted butter
- 1 tsp. parsley
- 1 tsp. minced garlic
- 1 shallot, minced
- 1 tbsp. Worcestershire sauce
- 1 tbsp. capers
- 1 tbsp. fresh lemon juice
- ¼ cup white wine

A GRATING OF FRESH PARMESAN CHEESE AND CAPERS PROVIDE A WONDERFUL FLAVOR ADDITION TO THIS DISH.

DIRECTIONS

In a food processor fitted with a stainless steel blade, pulse chop the cracker crumbs to produce an almost flour-like product.

Dip the venison cutlet in the beaten egg, then the cracker crumbs, coating both sides. Gently shake off excess cracker crumbs and place on a staging tray.

In a heavy skillet, melt ½ the butter over medium heat and quickly sauté the venison cutlets until they are golden brown on each side, 30 seconds to 1 minute per side. Remove to a paper towel lined pan and hold in a warm oven.

With a paper towel, carefully remove any cracker crumbs from the sauté pan. Reduce heat to low. Melt the remaining butter and quickly sauté the shallot and garlic. Stir in the parsley, Worcestershire sauce, capers, lemon juice and white wine. Increase heat to medium, bring to a boil and turn off heat.

Plate 2 venison cutlets per person. Spoon 1 tablespoon sauce over each and serve with steamed vegetables.

NEW ENGLAND VENISON ROAST

 SERVES 6–8

INGREDIENTS

- 4 lb. venison roast
- ½ tsp. salt
- ⅛ tsp. black pepper
- 4 medium potatoes, quartered
- 5 carrots, peeled and cut into 2" pieces
- 2 large onions, peeled and cut into 8 wedges each
- 2 stalks celery, thickly sliced
- 1 small head of cabbage, cut into 8 wedges
- 3 tbsp. red wine vinegar
- 1 bay leaf
- 1 can beer
- 3 cups beef stock

SAUCE

- 3 tbsp. flour
- 3 tbsp. butter
- 1 tbsp. onion soup mix
- 1½ cup reserved cooking liquid
- 1–2 tsp. prepared horseradish

DIRECTIONS

Place onion, carrots and celery in the bottom of a slow cooker. Season the venison with salt and pepper and place on top of the vegetables. Add the beer, beef stock and vinegar. Cover and cook on low 6–8 hours or until venison is tender. Remove and reserve 1½ cup cooking liquid for the sauce. Remove the venison, cover and keep warm.

Turn the slow cooker to high heat. Add the cabbage and potatoes and cook for 15–20 minutes or until cabbage and potatoes are tender.

Prepare the sauce. In a small saucepan, melt the butter and whisk in the flour. Whisk in the soup mix and then slowly wisk in the reserved cooking liquid. Add the horseradish and continue cooking, stirring constantly, until thickened.

Slice and plate the venison roast and vegetables. Serve the sauce on the side.

VENISON WITH PEPPERS AND PASTA

SERVES 6–8

INGREDIENTS

- 1 lb. venison steak, sliced across the grain and cut into bite-sized pieces
- 1 red bell pepper, seeded and sliced
- 1 green bell pepper, seeded and sliced
- Olive oil

MARINADE

- 2½ tbsp. teriyaki sauce
- 2½ tbsp. orange juice
- ½ tsp. black pepper
- ¼ tsp. thyme
- ½ tsp. granulated garlic
- 3 tbsp. sliced green onion
- Grated fresh ginger to taste (¼ tsp. if using dry ginger)
- 1 tsp. sesame oil

- 4 cups cooked ziti or mostaciolli tossed with ⅓ cup golden Italian dressing

> MARINATING THE VENISON OVERNIGHT MAKES FOR A MUCH MORE ROBUST FLAVOR.

DIRECTIONS

In a medium stainless steel bowl, wisk together the marinade ingredients. Add the venison, cover and refrigerate for at least 1 hour.

Heat a large sauté pan over high heat with a small amount of olive oil. Remove the venison from the marinade and place in the skillet. Sear until browned on all sides, 5–8 minutes. Stir in the peppers, reduce heat to low. Cover and cook until peppers are tender crisp. Add venison to the hot pasta. Toss and serve.

VENISON WITH PEPPERS AND PEA PODS

 SERVES 6–8

INGREDIENTS

- 2 lbs. boneless venison
- 3 tbsp. vegetable oil
- 2 tsp. minced garlic
- ¼ tsp. white pepper
- ⅓ cup teriyaki sauce
- 12 tbsp. brown sugar
- ¼ tsp. ground ginger
- 1 cup water
- 1 15-oz. can bean sprouts, drained
- 1 15-oz. can sliced stewed tomatoes
- 1 green bell pepper, seeded and cut into strips
- 1 red bell pepper, seeded and cut into strips
- 1 package frozen pea pods, thawed
- 5–6 green onions, sliced
- 1 tbsp. cornstarch
- 3 tbsp. water

YOU CAN SUBSTITUTE
GREEN BEANS OR
SHREDDED CHINESE
CABBAGE FOR THE
PEA PODS.

DIRECTIONS

Slice venison into narrow strips about 2" long. In a large skillet or sauté pan, heat the oil and brown the venison in batches over medium-high heat. Transfer the venison to a slow cooker. Add the garlic, white pepper, teriyaki sauce, ginger, sugar and 1 cup water. Cover and cook on low 6–8 hours. Turn heat to high, add peppers, pea pods and tomatoes. Cook 10 minutes, then stir in the cornstarch mixed with the 3 tablespoons of water. Continue cooking until thickened.

Serve on steamed rice garnished with sliced green onion.

VENISON ROULADEN

SERVES 6-8

INGREDIENTS

- 2 lbs. thinly sliced venison loin
- Bacon strips for rolling
- ½ cup dry red wine
- 1 cup beef stock
- 1 cup chopped parsley
- 1 cup chopped carrot

STUFFING

- 4 oz. ground venison
- 4 oz. ground pork or Italian sausage
- 3 tbsp. breadcrumbs
- ½ cup diced mushrooms
- ½ cup minced onion

DIRECTIONS

Thoroughly blend stuffing ingredients.

Pound venison slices between pieces of wax paper. Spread with stuffing and roll up. Wrap each roll with one strip of bacon secured with a toothpick. Arrange in a heavy baking dish. Over medium-low heat, brown on all sides until bacon is cooked. Add remaining ingredients and simmer until tender, approximately 1 hour. Remove toothpicks before serving.

SERVE OVER MASHED POTATOES OR WIDE EGG NOODLES.
IF YOU'D LIKE, YOU CAN STRAIN THE COOKING LIQUID
AND THICKEN IT FOR A DELICIOUS GRAVY.

VENISON, VERY DRY WITH AN OLIVE

 SERVES 6

INGREDIENTS

- **2–3 lb. venison roast**
- **3 tbsp. olive oil**
- **1 tbsp. black and white peppercorns, crushed**
- **2 medium onions, sliced**
- **2 15-oz. cans sliced stewed tomatoes**
- **1 cup beef broth**
- **1 tbsp. Worcestershire sauce**
- **1 tbsp. fines herbs**
- **½ cup heavy cream**
- **2 tbsp. dry vermouth**
- **2 tbsp. vodka**
- **½ cup pimento-stuffed olives**

FOR THE ADVENTUROUS
SPIRIT, TRY USING GARLIC
OR ANCHOVY
STUFFED OLIVES.

DIRECTIONS

Sprinkle the venison roast with the crushed peppercorns and salt to taste. In a heavy 4–6 quart dutch oven, heat the oil and brown the roast on all sides. Remove the venison to a holding tray. Add the onions to the dutch oven and stir until crisp. Add the venison, tomatoes, beef broth, Worcestershire sauce and fines herbs. Bring to a boil, reduce heat and simmer, covered, for 2–3 hours until venison is tender.

Remove roast from pan and let stand 10–15 minutes. Add cream, vermouth and vodka to the liquid in the dutch oven. Bring to a boil and remove immediately from the heat. Slice the roast, place on a serving platter and garnish with the sauce and olives.

VENISON WITH ZINFANDEL AND DRIED CRANBERRIES

 SERVES 6–8

INGREDIENTS

- ½ lb. bacon, cut crosswise into ½" pieces and sautéed until almost crisp
- 3 lb. venison roast, sprinkled with ¼ cup flour
- ¼ cup olive oil
- 1 tsp. minced garlic
- 4 white and 4 black peppercorns, crushed
- 1 bay leaf
- ½ tsp. Italian seasoning
- ½ tsp. thyme, crushed
- 2 medium onions, sliced and quartered
- 2 cups quartered mushrooms
- ½ cup dried cranberries
- 2 cups peeled and sliced carrots
- 2 cups sliced celery
- 1 bottle Zinfandel wine
- 3 tbsp. beef base
- 1 cup water
- 6 medium potatoes, peeled and cut into 1" dice
- Salt and pepper to taste

THIS DISH WILL
CERTAINLY IMPRESS
THE IN-LAWS.

DIRECTIONS

Using a heavy dutch oven, heat the olive oil. Cut the venison roast into 2 pieces. Dredge the cut ends in flour and brown on all sides. Transfer the venison to a slow cooker and add the bacon, garlic, peppercorns, bay leaf, Italian seasoning and thyme.

In a small bowl, dissolve the beef base in the water and add to the venison along with ½ bottle of the wine. Simmer for 3–4 hours on low heat or until the roast is tender. Remove venison and place in a pan to cool. Adjust the seasoning of the sauce with salt and pepper. Add carrots, celery, potatoes, onion, dried cranberries and remaining wine.

Increase heat to medium and cook until vegetables are tender, about 1 hour. Add the mushrooms for the last 15 minutes of cooking time.

Slice the venison roast and arrange on an ovenproof serving platter. Keep warm in a 150 degree oven.

To serve, remove venison from the oven. Arrange the vegetables around the venison and spoon sauce over all. Serve extra sauce at the table.

ROAST VENISON LOIN
A LA FRANKFURT

 SERVES 6-8

INGREDIENTS

- 4–6 lb. venison loin
- Salt and pepper to taste
- 4–6 thick slices bacon
- 2 tbsp. butter
- 1 large onion, peeled, cut in half and sliced
- 1 cup beef stock
- 1 cup sour cream
- ¼ cup heavy cream
- 1 lemon, thinly sliced
- 1 tsp. lemon juice
- 1 cup red wine
- 1 tbsp. flour
- 1 tbsp. butter

DIRECTIONS

Preheat oven to 400 degrees. Season the venison with salt and pepper. Wrap the roast with bacon and secure with toothpicks or kitchen string.

In a deep ovenproof sauté pan, melt the butter and brown the bacon-wrapped roast on all sides. Add the onion and beef stock, reduce heat to low. Cover and cook 40–45 minutes. Baste with cooking liquid and place in oven, uncovered, until bacon is almost crisp, 15–20 minutes.

Transfer roast to a cutting board and tent with foil to keep warm.

In a 1-quart saucepan, melt the butter, whisk in the flour and cook 1–2 minutes. Whisk in the heavy cream, sour cream, red wine and continue stirring until thickened. Stir in the onions and drippings from the sauté pan. Add beef stock if sauce is too thick. Adjust flavor with salt and pepper.

Remove toothpicks or string from roast. Slice and transfer to a heated serving platter and garnish with lemon slices. Serve the sauce on the side.

VENISON MEDALLIONS WITH PORT WINE AND LINGONBERRIES

 SERVES 6–8

INGREDIENTS

- 8 3–4 oz. venison tenderloin medallions
- ½ cup flour
- ⅛ tsp. white pepper
- ⅛ tsp. salt
- 2 grates fresh nutmeg
- ⅓ cup olive oil
- ½ lb. shiitake mushrooms, stemmed and sliced ½" thick
- ½ tsp. dried thyme
- ½ tsp. dried marjoram
- 1 cup chicken stock
- ½ cup port wine
- 2–3 tablespoons lingonberries
- 1½ cup heavy cream

FRESH HERBS WILL ENHANCE THE FLAVOR OF THIS DISH. CHOP AND ADD TO THE REDUCED SAUCE AT THE LAST MINUTE.

DIRECTIONS

In a gallon size plastic bag, mix together the flour, pepper, salt and nutmeg. Add the venison medallions, a few at a time, and thoroughly coat. Shake off extra flour and transfer to a holding plate.

In a large sauté pan or skillet, heat the olive oil over medium heat and sauté the medallions 2–3 minutes per side (medium rare). Add the mushrooms. Reduce heat to low and sauté for 3 minutes. Transfer the venison and mushrooms to a holding plate and cover to keep warm.

Add the thyme and marjoram to the sauté pan. Add the port wine and flame for no more than 20–30 seconds. Extinguish the flame with the pan cover. Stir in the chicken stock and lingonberries and reduce by half over high heat. Reduce the heat to low and stir in the cream. Continue stirring until thickened. Adjust seasoning to taste with salt and pepper. Serve the medallions topped with the sauce reduction.

VENISON FAJITAS

SERVES 6–8

INGREDIENTS

- 1 lb. venison roast sliced ½" thick and cut into strips
- 1 large onion, peeled, cut in half and sliced ½" thick
- 1 red bell pepper, seeded and cut into strips
- 1 green bell pepper, seeded and cut into strips
- 4 tbsp. olive oil

SPICE MIX

- 2 tsp. chili powder
- 1 tsp. cumin
- 1 tsp. dried oregano
- ½ tsp. granulated garlic (optional)
- 1 tsp. sugar

PACKAGE AND
FREEZE THE
FAJITA MIXTURE
FOR A QUICK
MEAL OR SNACK.

DIRECTIONS

Combine the Spice Mix ingredients and divide into 2 portions

In a large bowl, toss the venison strips with 1 portion of the spice mix. Cover and refrigerate for at least 1 hour.

Preheat a heavy fry pan to medium-high heat. Add 2 tablespoons olive oil and fry the venison in 2 batches until brown on all sides. Place venison in a shallow baking pan and keep warm in a preheated 250 degree oven.

Preheat the fry pan with high heat. Add 2 tablespoons olive oil. When very hot, carefully add the peppers and onion and sprinkle with the remaining spice mix. Cook until tender and crisp, 5–6 minutes. Add the venison to the peppers and onions. Toss and serve with warmed tortillas, sour cream, salsa, shredded cheese and shredded lettuce.

HUNGARIAN VENISON PAPRIKASH

INGREDIENTS

- 2 lbs. venison steak, cut into bite-size pieces
- 1 medium onion, thinly sliced
- 1 medium green pepper, cut into ¼" strips
- 1 15-oz. can stewed tomatoes
- 2 tbsp. Hungarian sweet paprika
- ½ cup chicken broth
- 1 tbsp. flour
- ¾ cup sour cream
- Olive oil

DIRECTIONS

In a large nonstick skillet over medium-high heat, cook the venison in 1 tablespoon olive oil until lightly browned on all sides.

Reduce heat to medium and add the onion pepper and paprika to the skillet. Cook and stir until the onion is soft. Sprinkle flour over the venison/vegetable mixture and stir for 1 minute. Add the tomatoes and chicken stock and cook 3–4 minutes or until the sauce is slightly thickened. Slowly stir in the sour cream and heat for 1–2 minutes. Adjust seasoning as desired. Serve over buttered noodles.

AS A VARIATION, ADD COOKED DICED
POTATOES, CARROTS AND PEAS WHEN
YOU ADD THE SOUR CREAM.

MEDITERRANEAN VENISON

SERVES 6–8

INGREDIENTS

- 2 lb. boneless venison short loin
- 1 tbsp. olive oil
- 1 tbsp. minced garlic, mixed with 2 tbsp. butter

MEDITERRANEAN SPICE RUB

Process the following in a spice grinder:

- 2 tsp. salt
- 1 tbsp. oregano
- 1 tbsp. granulated garlic
- 1 tsp. dried lemon peel
- ⅛ tsp. black pepper
- ⅛ tsp. white pepper

LEFTOVERS CAN BE
THINLY SLICED AND
USED IN A WONDERFUL
ENTRÉE SALAD. STORE
ANY UNUSED SPICE
RUB IN A COVERED
CONTAINER.

DIRECTIONS

Preheat oven to 400 degrees.

Rub venison with olive oil and 1 tablespoon of the spice rub. Place on a rack in a baking pan and roast for 10 minutes. Spread the garlic butter on the top of the roast. Return the venison to the oven and continue roasting until the internal temperature reaches 125 degrees. Transfer to a cutting board and tent with foil. Allow to rest 10 minutes before carving.

VENISON STROGANOFF

SERVES 6–8

INGREDIENTS

- 2 lbs. venison tenderloin, cut into ½" strips, 2" long
- 8 oz. button mushrooms, quartered
- 1 large onion, thickly sliced and cut in half
- 2 cups beef broth
- 2 tbsp. cornstarch
- 2 tbsp. tomato paste
- ¼ cup cream sherry
- 1 tsp. Dijon mustard
- ¼ lb. unsalted butter
- ⅛ tsp. crushed dried marjoram
- ½ cup sour cream

IF YOU ARE WATCHING YOUR CALORIES, SUBSTITUTE LOW FAT YOGURT FOR THE SOUR CREAM.

DIRECTIONS

In a large heavy skillet melt 2 tablespoons butter over medium heat. Add the venison and stir fry for 1 minute. Add the mushrooms and onions and the remaining 2 tablespoons butter. Cook for 2–3 minutes until onion is soft.

In a bowl, whisk together the cornstarch, tomato paste, sherry and mustard. Slowly add the beef broth, wisking until completely blended.

Sprinkle the marjoram on the cooked venison. Reduce heat to low and slowly stir in the cornstarch mixture. Simmer for 3–4 minutes or until thickened.

Add 1 cup of the hot cooking liquid from the skillet to the sour cream and mix thoroughly. Add this mixture to the skillet and stir to blend well. Cook for an additional 3–4 minutes, stirring occasionally. Serve over buttered noodles or steamed rice.

VENISON SHOULDER ROAST
WITH BREAD STUFFING

SERVES 4–6

INGREDIENTS

- 4 lb. boned shoulder roast, butterflied
- ½ tsp. salt
- ¼ tsp. white pepper
- 4 oz. butter
- 1 medium onion, peeled, sliced and chopped
- 4 oz. fresh mushrooms, sliced
- 3 stalks celery, finely sliced
- 2 cloves garlic, crushed and minced
- ⅓ cup fresh parsley, chopped
- ½ tsp. marjoram
- 3 cups seasoned breadcrumbs
- 1 large egg, beaten
- ¼ cup dried cranberries
- 4 large carrots, peeled
- 1 large onion, peeled and cut into 8 wedges
- 2 cups chicken stock

VENISON AND FRUIT ARE NATURAL COMPANIONS.
ADD DRIED APPLES OR APRICOTS TO YOUR STUFFING IF
DESIRED—BE SURE TO SOAK THEM IN SHERRY FIRST.

DIRECTIONS

Season the venison with salt and pepper and place skin side down on a holding tray. Cover and refrigerate.

In a large sauté pan, melt the butter. Stir in the mushroom, onion, celery and garlic. Cook for 10 minutes. Mix in the parsley and marjoram. Transfer to a large bowl and combine with the breadcrumbs, egg, and dried cranberries. Spread stuffing mix on the butterflied roast, roll up and tie with kitchen twine.

Place the carrots on the bottom of a roasting pan. Place the roast on top of the carrots and arrange the onion wedges around the sides of the roast. Cook in a 425 degree oven for 25 minutes. Reduce heat to 325 degrees and add 1 cup chicken stock. Cover and bake 2–2½ hours, basting frequently and adding more chicken stock as needed. Remove cover for the last 20 minutes.

Let the roast stand for 15 minutes and remove the twine before carving. Strain the pan juices and serve on the side, thickening if desired.

GROUND VENISON

BREAKFAST SKILLET

 SERVES 4–6

INGREDIENTS

- 1 lb. ground venison
- 8 strips bacon, chopped
- ½ tsp. smoked paprika
- ⅛ tsp. white pepper
- 2 cups hash brown potatoes, raw
- 6 oz. small curd cottage cheese
- 6 oz. mixed shredded cheeses
  (cheddar, mozzarella, Monterey jack)
- 7 eggs, beaten

A GREAT DISH FOR A
BRUNCH. IF YOU'D LIKE,
SPICE IT UP A BIT BY
SERVING ANY KIND OF
SALSA ON THE SIDE.

DIRECTIONS

In a large skillet or sauté pan, brown the bacon over medium heat. Stir in the venison, paprika and pepper. Cook and stir until the venison is no longer pink. Drain the mixture in a sieve.

In a large bowl, combine all ingredients. Transfer to a buttered baking dish. Bake in a 325 degree oven 40–60 minutes until set and browned.

VENISON BREAKFAST WRAP

INGREDIENTS

- 1 10" flour tortilla
- Chili powder to taste
- 2 eggs
- 2 tsp. butter
- 2 tbsp. finely minced onion
- 2 tbsp. finely minced bell pepper
- 4 tbsp. ground venison (browned)
- 3 tbsp. shredded cheese
- 1–2 tbsp. sour cream
- 2–3 tbsp. salsa

DIRECTIONS

In a 6–8" nonstick skillet or omelet pan, melt butter over medium heat. Whisk eggs with a sprinkling of chili powder. Pour eggs into skillet and swirl to distribute the mixture evenly. Cook for 1–2 minutes or until eggs are almost set. Sprinkle onion, green pepper and venison over the eggs. Remove from heat and sprinkle with cheese. Cover for 1–2 minutes. Slide the egg "pancake" onto the warmed tortilla, roll up and fold like a burrito. Slice in half and serve with sour cream and salsa.

IF COOKING FOR A CROWD, COMPLETED WRAPS CAN BY ARRANGED IN A SHALLOW BAKING DISH AND HELD COVERED IN A 225 DEGREE OVEN FOR 30–45 MINUTES.

BURGERS WITH BACON AND CHEDDAR CHEESE

SERVES 8

INGREDIENTS
- 2 lbs. ground venison
- ½ lb. bacon, sliced and chopped
- 1 medium onion, sliced and finely chopped
- 8 oz. shredded sharp cheddar cheese
- 1 egg, beaten
- 1 tbsp. Worcestershire sauce
- ½ tsp. onion powder

DIRECTIONS
To transform this recipe into a paté for hors d'oeuvres—place all ingredients in a food processor and pulse chop 5–6 times, adding 1 additional egg. Place in a loaf pan and bake at 325 degrees 45–50 minutes. Chill and slice. Serve with crackers or garlic toast.

In a heavy skillet, sauté the bacon over medium heat until slightly opaque. Add the onion and stir until onion is translucent. Strain to remove excess bacon fat and cool to room temperature.

In a large bowl, mix all ingredients by hand. Divide the mixture into 8 portions, form into patties and grill or fry to your desired degree of doneness. Serve on toasted Kaiser rolls.

GERMAN STYLE GROUND VENISON

INGREDIENTS

- **2 lb. ground venison**
- **3–4 bratwurst, cooked and sliced ⅜" thick**
- **1 medium onion, peeled, sliced and chopped**
- **2 tbsp. butter**
- **¼ tsp. seasoned salt**
- **¼ tsp. black pepper**
- **¼ tsp. ground fennel**
- **1 tbsp. flour**
- **2 tsp. paprika**
- **4-oz. can tomato sauce**
- **1 cup sour cream**
- **1 tbsp. dried parsley**

THIS DISH IS VERY RICH. TO REDUCE THE CALORIES, SUBSTITUTE LOW FAT YOGURT FOR THE SOUR CREAM AND SMOKED PAPRIKA FOR THE PAPRIKA.

DIRECTIONS

In a large sauté pan, heat the butter and cook the onion for 3–4 minutes. Add the venison and cook over medium heat, stirring, until browned. Add the bratwurst, salt, pepper, fennel, paprika and tomato sauce. Mix well. Cover and reduce heat to low. Cook for 20–30 minutes. Stir in the sour cream mixed with the flour and heat until thickened. Adjust seasoning to taste. Sprinkle with parsley and serve over boiled potatoes.

FRITTATA

SERVES 6–8

INGREDIENTS
- 1 lb. ground venison

SEASONING MIX
- ⅛ tsp. crushed oregano
- ⅛ tsp. white pepper
- ⅛ tsp. salt
- ⅛ tsp. nutmeg
- ⅛ tsp. ground cumin
- ⅛ tsp. granulated garlic
- 2 tbsp. olive
- 1½ lb. medium russet potatoes, peeled and sliced ¼" thick
- 1 large onion, peeled, sliced ½" thick and cut in half
- 1 green bell pepper, seeded and cut in ½" strips
- 1 red bell pepper, seeded and cut in ½" strips
- 2 tbsp. olive oil
- 8 eggs, beaten with ¼ cup heavy cream
- 1 tsp. smoked paprika
- ½ tsp. salt
- ½ cup grated cheddar cheese

RESERVE A FEW PEPPER STRIPS TO DECORATE
THE TOP OF THE FRITTATA BEFORE BAKING.
THIS DISH IS ALSO WONDERFUL SERVED COLD
OR AT ROOM TEMPERATURE.

DIRECTIONS

Preheat oven to 325 degrees.

In a large bowl, mix together the venison and seasoning mix. Cover and refrigerate 20–30 minutes.

In a heavy sauté pan, heat 2 tablespoons olive oil and brown the venison. Remove from the sauté pan and allow to cool. Add the remaining 2 tablespoons olive oil to the sauté pan along with the onions and cook until they are golden. Stir in the peppers, reduce heat to low, cover and cook, covered, until the peppers are tender crisp, about 3 minutes. Remove the peppers and onions to a bowl to cool.

Place the sliced potatoes in a 3–4 quart pan. Cover with water 3" above the potatoes and bring to a boil. Reduce heat and cook until just tender, 6–8 minutes. Drain potatoes, rinse in cold water and allow to cool.

Spray or butter a 9x12" glass baking dish. Arrange the potato slices in concentric layers, starting at the center of the dish. Cover the potatoes with the browned venison, peppers, and onions and top with the cheese. Mix the paprika and salt with the egg and cream mixture. Pour over the ingredients in the baking dish. Bake for 40–45 minutes until a knife inserted in the center comes out clean and the eggs are totally set.

Allow the frittata to cool for 15–20 minutes before serving.

INDIVIDUAL MEATLOAVES

 SERVES 8

INGREDIENTS
- 3 lbs. ground venison
- 1 lb. raw breakfast or Italian sausage
- 2 egg yolks
- 2 oz. melted butter
- ½ cup breadcrumbs
- 1 can tomato soup

CAN BE USED AS A
DINNER ENTRÉE OR
SLICE AND MAKE
SANDWICHES.

DIRECTIONS
In a large bowl, mix all ingredients except the tomato soup. Divide into 8 equal portions and shape into individual loafs. Top each with 1 tablespoon of the tomato soup concentrate.

Bake in a 325 degree oven for 20–30 minutes or until a meat thermometer reads 160 degrees. Serve with mashed potatoes and mixed vegetables.

ITALIAN MEATBALLS

INGREDIENTS

- 2 slices bread soaked in ½ cup milk
- 1½ lb. ground venison
- ½ lb. raw bulk Italian sausage (sweet or hot)
- 2 eggs, beaten
- 2 tbsp. butter
- ½ cup minced onion
- 2 tsp. chopped garlic
- 3 tbsp. chopped parsley
- ½ tsp. salt
- ¼ tsp. paprika
- 1 tsp. lemon juice
- 4 tbsp. grated Parmesan cheese
- ½ tsp. crushed oregano
- 1 jar marinara sauce

THESE MEATBALLS ARE EXTREMELY VERSATILE AND WILL ACCEPT MANY DIFFERENT FLAVORS (SEE THAI MEATBALL RECIPE).

DIRECTIONS

Squeeze the milk from the bread. In a food processor, combine the bread with the sausage and venison. Pulse chop to combine. Transfer to a large bowl. Mix in the beaten egg, onion, cheese and all spices. Form into balls 1" in diameter (approximately ½ ounce).

In a large skillet, melt the butter and brown the meatballs on all sides. Transfer to a baking dish. Top with the marinara sauce, cover and bake in a 325 degree oven for 30–40 minutes.

KONIGSBERGER KLOPSE
(GERMAN MEATBALLS)

 SERVES 4

INGREDIENTS

- 2 slices bread soaked in ½ cup milk
- 1 lb. ground venison
- ½ lb. ground pork
- 2 eggs
- 1 tbsp. butter
- ⅓ cup minced onion
- 3 tbsp. chopped parsley
- ½ tsp. salt
- ¼ tsp. paprika
- ⅓ tsp. fresh lemon zest, chopped
- 1 tbsp. lemon juice
- 1 tbsp. Worcestershire sauce
- 4 anchovy filets, finely chopped (optional)
- Sprinkling of nutmeg
- 6 cups chicken or vegetable stock

THESE MEATBALLS ARE ALSO GREAT AS AN APPETIZER—
REDUCE THE SIZE TO 1" (ABOUT 1 OUNCE).

DIRECTIONS

Squeeze the milk from the bread. In a food processor, combine the pork, venison and bread. Pulse chop 3–5 times to combine. Transfer to a large bowl.

In a large skillet, melt the butter and sauté the onion until golden brown. Add to the meat mixture with the remaining ingredients except for the chicken or vegetable stock. Combine well using your impeccably clean hands. Shape into 2" balls. Drop into the boiling stock and simmer, covered, for 15 minutes.

Transfer the meatballs to a baking dish.

The Gravy: For every cup of stock to be made into gravy, prepare the following: In a large skillet, melt 2 tablespoons butter. Whisk in 2 tablespoons flour, cooking and whisking until smooth and thickened. Stir in the cooking liquid, cooking over low heat until thickened. Add 2 tablespoons finely chopped capers and ½ cup sour cream.

Place meatballs in the gravy and reheat over low heat for 15 minutes. Serve over buttered noodles.

MEATLOAF A LA REUBEN

SERVES 8

INGREDIENTS

- 2 lb. ground venison
- 1 cup rye bread, cut into small cubes
- 1 medium onion, peeled, sliced and minced
- 3 tbsp. sweet pickle relish
- 1 large egg, beaten
- ¼ tsp. granulated garlic
- ¼ tsp. salt
- ⅛ tsp. white pepper
- ⅓ cup thousand island dressing
- 8 oz. fresh sauerkraut, rinsed and drained
- 5 oz. shredded Swiss cheese

FOR A SHARPER
RYE FLAVOR, ADD
1/4 TSP. CRUSHED
CARAWAY SEEDS.

DIRECTIONS

In a food processor fitted with a metal blade, pulse chop the venison and rye bread until combined. Add the onion, relish, egg, garlic, salt and pepper and pulse chop until thoroughly mixed. Spray a 12x16" piece of heavy duty foil with cooking spray. Spread the venison mixture in a 10x14" rectangle on the foil. Top with the dressing, sauerkraut and 4 ounces of the Swiss cheese.

Using the foil as an aid, create a 14" long "jelly roll" sealing the ends and side seam. Carefully transfer the roll to a sprayed 15x10" baking pan. Bake uncovered at 325 degrees 50–60 minutes or until the internal temperature reaches 160 degrees. Sprinkle top with 1 ounce of Swiss cheese and bake until cheese is melted. Let stand 10–15 minutes before serving.

MEATLOAF

INGREDIENTS

- 2 lbs. ground venison
- 6 slices bacon, chopped in a food processor
- 1 medium onion, minced
- 2 large eggs
- 1 cup ketchup
- ½ cup bread or cracker crumbs
- ½ tsp. mild chili powder
- ½ tsp. chopped garlic
- ¼ tsp. white pepper

DIRECTIONS

In a large bowl, mix together all ingredients. Bake in a loaf pan in a pre-heated 325 degree oven for 45–60 minutes until temperature in the center of the loaf reaches 160 degrees. Serve with mashed potatoes and a steamed and buttered green vegetable.

TO SPICE THINGS UP, USE A MIXTURE OF 1/2 CUP
KETCHUP AND 1/2 CUP SPICY SALSA OR ADD A SMALL
MINCED JALAPEÑO PEPPER TO THE MEATLOAF MIXTURE.

MOSTACIOLLI

INGREDIENTS

- 8 oz. whole grain mostaciolli noodles, cooked
- 4 cups venison spaghetti sauce
- 3 medium zucchini, sliced and quartered
- 3 yellow squash, sliced and quartered
- 1 cup black olives, sliced
- 4 cups shredded Italian cheese (asiago, mozzarella, Romano, provolone)

THE PERFECT WAY TO INTRODUCE YOUR FAMILY AND FRIENDS TO WHOLE GRAIN PASTA.

DIRECTIONS

Coat a 9x13" baking pan with cooking spray (the deeper the pan, the better). Spread 1 cup of sauce on the bottom of the pan. Top with ⅓ of the pasta, ⅓ of the vegetables, ⅓ of the olives and ¼ of the cheese. Repeat layers. Top layers should be sauce and cheese.

Bake in a preheated 325 degree oven for 30–40 minutes, or until the cheese is melted and the sauce is bubbly. Remove from oven and let sit 20 minutes before serving.

QUICK STROGANOFF

INGREDIENTS

- 1½ lb. ground venison
- 3 tbsp. butter
- 1 medium onion, peeled, sliced and chopped
- 1 tsp. garlic
- 1 tbsp. flour
- 2 chicken bouillon cubes, dissolved in ¼ cup hot water
- 1 can condensed cream of mushroom soup
- 1 cup milk or cream
- ¼ lb. mushrooms, sliced
- 8 oz. sour cream mixed with 2 tsp. paprika
- 1 lb. package wide egg noodles, cooked according to package directions

DIRECTIONS

In a large skillet over medium heat, melt the butter and brown the venison. Stir in the onion and garlic and cook until the onion is opaque. Stir in the flour, milk, soup, bouillon and mushrooms and mix well. Bring to a boil and reduce heat. Simmer 10–15 minutes. Stir in the sour cream and continue cooking until heated through. Serve over hot buttered noodles.

QUICK, EASY AND TASTY. A PERFECT RECIPE TO USE IN
TEACHING YOUR CHILDREN BASIC COOKING TECHNIQUES.

RAGOUT

SERVES 4

INGREDIENTS

- 1 lb. ground venison
- 2 tbsp. olive oil
- 1 large onion, peeled, sliced and chopped
- 3 stalks celery, sliced and chopped
- 2 carrots, peeled, sliced and chopped
- ¼ lb. bacon, chopped
- 1 cup chicken stock
- 1 15-oz. can stewed tomatoes, drained and chopped
- 1 tbsp. minced garlic, about 3 cloves
- Dash white pepper
- 1 tsp. dried oregano, crushed
- ⅓ cup white wine
- 10 oz. spaghetti or other long pasta, cooked according to package directions

DIRECTIONS

In a large heavy skillet or sauté pan, heat 1 tablespoon olive oil and sauté the venison for 3–5 minutes until no longer pink. Transfer to a 2–3 quart dutch oven. Reheat the skillet, add the remaining olive oil and sauté the onion, celery and carrot until tender, 5–6 minutes. Transfer to the dutch oven and stir in the bacon, stewed tomatoes, garlic, chicken stock, oregano and pepper. Cover and cook over medium low heat 25–30 minutes. Stir in the wine and adjust seasoning to taste. Cook 10 minutes more. Serve over cooked and drained pasta.

FOR THOSE WHO PREFER SPICY FOODS,
SERVE CRUSHED RED PEPPER ON THE SIDE.

SPAGHETTI SAUCE

INGREDIENTS

- 2 lbs. ground venison
- 1 lb. fresh Italian sausage (sweet or hot)
- 1 can chicken stock
- 2 15-oz. cans stewed tomatoes, sliced
- 1 small can tomato paste
- 2 medium onions, diced
- 2 cans chopped clams (optional)
- 2 medium green peppers, seeded and diced
- 3 cloves garlic, minced
- 3 stalks celery, diced
- 10 fresh mushrooms, sliced
- 2 tsp. Italian seasoning
- ¼ tsp. crushed red pepper
- 2 tbsp. brown sugar
- ¼ cup golden Italian dressing

THE ADDITION OF CHOPPED CLAMS ROUNDS OUT AND ENHANCES THE FLAVOR OF THIS SAUCE.

DIRECTIONS

Lightly oil a large sauté pan. Over medium heat, cook the onions, garlic, celery and peppers until soft. Place in a 4-quart stockpot.

In the sauté pan, brown the Italian sausage and the venison. Place in the stockpot. Over medium heat, add the tomatoes, tomato paste and chicken stock, stirring well. Add the Italian seasoning and dressing, the red pepper and brown sugar and clams (if desired).

Simmer 2½–3 hours, stirring occasionally. Add additional chicken stock if necessary. Adjust seasoning to taste with salt and pepper and brown sugar. Add the mushrooms and simmer an additional ½ hour. Serve over spaghetti.

SPICY VENISON AND EGGPLANT

 SERVES 6–8

INGREDIENTS

- 8 oz. ground venison
- 1 tbsp. teriyaki sauce
- 2 cups eggplant, peeled and cut into ¾" cubes
- 1 large onion, sliced thick and quartered
- ⅓ cup cream sherry
- 1 tbsp. sesame oil
- 3 tbsp. peanut oil
- 1 tbsp. minced garlic
- 1 tsp. oriental chili paste
- ½ tsp. minced fresh ginger
- chicken stock as needed

STIR FRY SAUCE

Mix together:
- 3 tbsp. oyster sauce
- 3 tbsp. teriyaki sauce
- 1 tsp. cornstarch
- 1 tsp. brown sugar

IF YOU ARE USING ORIENTAL CHILI PASTE FOR THE FIRST TIME, START WITH 0 T. THE CHILI PASTE INTENSIFIES IN FLAVOR WHEN COOKED. YOU CAN ALWAYS ADD MORE TO ADJUST THE FLAVOR TO YOUR LIKING.

DIRECTIONS

In a stainless steel bowl, mix the venison with the teriyaki sauce. Cover and refrigerate. Combine the sherry and sesame oil in a small bowl.

Heat a wok over high heat. Stir-fry garlic, ginger and chili paste in peanut oil for 20–30 seconds. Add the venison and stir-fry until browned. Add the eggplant and onion. Stir in the sherry and sesame seed oil mixture. Add chicken stock to bring the level of the liquid to ½ the level of the venison and eggplant.

Cover and cook over medium heat until the eggplant is tender, about 4–5 minutes. Add the stir-fry sauce. Turn heat to high and stir-fry until sauce thickens. Serve over steamed rice.

STUFFED BURGERS

SERVES 6

INGREDIENTS

- 2 slices bread soaked in ½ cup milk
- 1½ lb. ground venison
- ½ lb. ground pork or pork sausage
- 2 eggs, beaten
- ¼ tsp. smoked paprika
- 1 tbsp. Worcestershire sauce
- 6 strips thickly sliced bacon
- 3 oz. bleu or stilton cheese
- 3 oz. cream cheese
- 1 tbsp. minced capers
- Freshly ground pepper to taste

THESE BURGERS CAN BE CASUALLY SERVED ON A BUN OR ELEGANTLY SERVED WITH SAUCE BÉARNAISE.

DIRECTIONS

Squeeze the milk from the bread. In a food processor, combine the bread with the pork and venison. Pulse chop to combine. Transfer to a large bowl. Mix in the beaten egg, paprika and Worcestershire sauce. Divide into 6 balls, cut each in half and form into 3" diameter patties. Cover and refrigerate.

In a medium bowl, mix together the cheeses, capers and pepper. Transfer to a sheet of plastic wrap. Form into a cylinder 6" long. Wrap in the plastic wrap and put into freezer for at least 1 hour. Remove from freezer and cut into 6 equal portions.

Place a piece of the cheese mixture on a venison patty, top with a second patty. Form the venison so it completely covers the cheese. Wrap the patty with a strip of bacon. Fasten with a round toothpick.

Heat a large heavy skillet over medium-high heat. Melt 2 tablespoons butter. Add the burgers and brown on each side. Transfer to a baking dish. Bake in a 325 degree oven for 15 minutes.

VENISON TURBAN

INGREDIENTS

- 1 lb. ground venison
- 1 lb. ground pork or breakfast sausage
- 2 slices bread soaked in ½ cup milk
- 2 eggs, beaten
- ½ cup minced onion
- 1 tsp. smoked paprika
- 1 tsp. lemon zest, minced
- ¼ cup minute rice
- Leaves from 1 medium head of cabbage blanched until flexible

SAUCE

In a large saucepan, melt 2 tablespoons butter and wisk in 2 tablespoons flour over low heat. Add 2 cups chicken stock and 1 can condensed vegetable soup. Whisk until blended—add additional chicken stock to achieve desired consistency.

To serve, place the cheesecloth bag in a colander and drain for 2–3 minutes. Untie the bag and drape the cheesecloth ends over the sides of the colander. Invert the colander onto a hot serving plate. Slice the turban into wedges and serve the sauce on the side.

DIRECTIONS

Squeeze the milk from the bread. Place the bread, venison and pork in a food processor. Pulse chop until well blended.

Place the meat mixture in a large bowl and mix in by hand the eggs, onion, paprika, lemon zest and rice.

Line a large bowl with cheesecloth long enough to be gathered and tied when the bowl is filled. Line the bowl with blanched cabbage leaves. Add a 1" layer of the meat mixture covered with a single layer of cabbage leaves. Continue layering until all the meat mixture is used, ending with cabbage. Gather up the cheesecloth and tie securely with string.

In a medium stockpot, bring 4 quarts chicken stock to a boil. Carefully place the cheesecloth bag in the pot. Reduce heat to low and simmer for 2 hours, making sure the bag is always covered with stock.

IF THERE IS EXTRA CABBAGE, COOK IT IN THE POT WITH THE TURBAN FOR THE LAST 1/2 HOUR. SERVE IT BUTTERED AS A SIDE DISH.

STUFFED PEPPERS

SERVES 8

INGREDIENTS

- 8 medium green peppers, tops and seeds removed
- 1 lb. ground venison
- ¼ cup minced onion
- 1 cup cooked rice
- 2 eggs, well beaten
- ½ tsp. paprika
- ¼ tsp. celery salt
- ¼ tsp. thyme
- 8 strips crisp bacon
- ½ cup shredded cheddar cheese

A SIMPLE SAUCE CAN BE MADE WITH CONDENSED TOMATO SOUP PREPARED WITH MILK AND YOUR FAVORITE HERBS.

DIRECTIONS

Preheat oven to 350 degrees.

In a heavy skillet, sauté the onion in 2 tablespoons butter until translucent. Add the ground venison and stir until cooked, 3–5 minutes. Transfer to a large bowl and allow to cool. Stir in the rice, paprika, salt and thyme. Mix in the eggs and cheese. Fill each pepper with this mixture and top with 1 strip of bacon, crumbled.

Arrange filled peppers in a deep dutch oven, add ½" water, cover and bake 20 minutes or until pepper shells are tender and the cheese has melted. Serve with your favorite marinara sauce.

SWEET SOUR STUFFED CABBAGE

SERVES 6

INGREDIENTS

- 8 large blanched cabbage leaves
- 2 lbs. ground venison
- ½ cup minced onion
- 1 tbsp. chopped parsley
- ½ tsp. crushed thyme
- ⅛ tsp. pepper
- 2 tbsp. vinegar
- 3 tbsp. brown sugar
- 1 tbsp. finely chopped capers
- 1 egg, beaten
- 1 can vegetable soup
- 1 cup beef stock

FOR A RICHER
SAUCE, ADD 1 CUP
SOUR CREAM.

DIRECTIONS

In a large bowl, mix all ingredients except the cabbage, beef broth and vegetable soup.

Divide the meat mixture equally among the 8 cabbage leaves. Fold the leaves around the meat and secure with a round toothpick. Place seam-side down in a buttered baking dish. Mix the soup with water as directed on the can then mix with the beef stock. Pour the soup mixture over the stuffed cabbage. Cover and bake in a 325 degree oven for 40–50 minutes.

THAI COUNTRY-STYLE CURRY

INGREDIENTS

- 2 lbs. ground venison
- 2 tbsp. vegetable oil
- 1 cup chicken stock, mixed with
  1 tbsp. panang curry paste
- 2 tbsp. fish sauce
- 6 basil leaves, shredded
- 2 cups shredded cabbage
- 2 medium carrots, shredded
- 1–2 Thai chili peppers, minced (optional)
- 1 15-oz. can unsweetened coconut milk

THAI CHILI PEPPERS CAN BE CHOPPED AND STORED IN PLASTIC BAGS IN THE FREEZER.

DIRECTIONS

Heat the vegetable oil in a wok and stir-fry the venison for 3–4 minutes. Add the shredded cabbage and carrot, continue cooking for 4–5 minutes. Add the chili pepper (if desired) and stir in the chicken stock curry paste mixture and bring to a boil. Stir in basil leaves, reduce heat and simmer 3–5 minutes. Serve over steamed rice.

THAI MEATBALLS

INGREDIENTS

- 1 lb. Italian Meatballs (see recipe on page 99)
- 2 tbsp. red Thai curry paste
- ½ cup hot water
- 3 tbsp. brown sugar
- 1 cup ketchup
- ½ cup lime juice
- 1 cup teriyaki sauce
- 1 tsp. garlic, minced

AS AN HORS D'OEUVRE, THIS RECIPE WILL SERVE 6–8 GUESTS.

DIRECTIONS

Preheat oven to 325 degrees.

Place meatballs in baking dish. In a large bowl, wisk together the curry paste and hot water. Add the brown sugar, ketchup, lime juice, teriyaki sauce and garlic. Pour over meatballs, cover and bake for 20–30 minutes until hot and bubbly.

VENISON AND SPANISH RICE

SERVES 6–8

INGREDIENTS
- 3 cups cooked white rice
- 1 cup chopped onion
- 1 cup sliced celery
- 1 cup seeded and chopped green bell pepper
- 1 tbsp. butter
- 1½ lb. ground venison, seasoned with ¼ tsp. salt, 1 tbsp. smoked paprika and 1 tsp. chili powder
- 1 can condensed tomato soup
- 1 soup can of milk

GREAT DISH FOR A BUFFET OR FOR FEEDING A CROWD. RECIPE CAN BE DOUBLED OR TRIPLED WITHOUT PROBLEMS.

DIRECTIONS
Preheat oven to 325 degrees.

In a large heavy sauté pan or skillet, melt the butter. Add the onion and sauté until opaque. Add the seasoned venison and stir-fry for 3–4 minutes.

Using a greased 9x12" baking dish, layer 1 cup of rice, then ⅓ of the venison, then ⅓ of the celery and peppers. Repeat layers 2 more times. Top with soup diluted with 1 can of milk. Bake 25–30 minutes.

VENISON BBQ

SERVES 8

INGREDIENTS

- 2 lb. ground venison
- 2 tbsp. butter
- ½ cup chopped onion
- 1 cup chopped green bell pepper
- ½ cup sliced mushrooms
- ½ cup chili sauce
- ½ cup cranberry juice
- 1 tsp. chili powder

QUICK AND EASY DOWN HOME GOODNESS THAT WE ALL CRAVE.

DIRECTIONS

In a heavy sauté pan, melt the butter over medium heat. Add the onion and green pepper and cook until the onions are opaque. Add the venison and stir until the meat is browned. Add the mushrooms, chili sauce, cranberry juice and chili powder. Reduce heat to low and simmer until thickened, about 20 minutes. Serve on toasted buns.

VENISON AND CORNBREAD PIE

INGREDIENTS

- 1 lb. ground venison
- 1 large onion, chopped
- 2 large tomatoes, chopped
- 2 medium green peppers, seeded, sliced and chopped
- 1 tbsp. canola oil
- 1 package frozen whole kernel corn, thawed
- 1 cup chicken stock
- 1 tbsp. Worcestershire sauce
- 1 tsp. ground cumin
- 1 tsp. chili powder
- 2 tbsp. dark molasses

CORNBREAD

- 1½ cup yellow corn meal
- ¼ cup all-purpose flour
- 2 tsp. baking powder
- ¼ tsp. salt
- 1 tsp. brown sugar
- 3 egg whites
- ½ cup buttermilk
- 1 tbsp. melted butter
- ½ cup chopped green onion

FREEZE INDIVIDUAL SERVINGS FOR A QUICK,
HEARTY MEAL. CAN BE REHEATED
IN THE MICROWAVE.

DIRECTIONS

Preheat oven to 350 degrees.

Heat a large nonstick frypan over medium heat. Add the venison and stir fry for 3–4 minutes. Remove the cooked venison and drain any excess moisture. Return the pan to medium heat, add the oil and stir in the onion and pepper. Cook for 3–4 minutes, Add the corn and venison. Cook an additional 4–5 minutes. Stir in the Worcestershire sauce, spices and salt. Add the chicken stock and molasses. Reduce heat to low, cover and simmer for 15 minutes, stirring occasionally. Transfer the venison mixture to a 9x12" baking pan or dish.

In a large bowl, combine the cornmeal, flour, baking powder, salt and brown sugar. In a small bowl, wisk together the egg whites, buttermilk and melted butter. Stir this mixture into the cornmeal mixture. Fold in the green onion and stir gently to combine.

Top the venison mixture with the cornbread mixture. Bake for 30–45 minutes or until the cornmeal is golden brown.

VENISON DUMPLINGS BOLOGNESE

SERVES 6–8

INGREDIENTS

- 1½ lb. ground venison
- 6 oz. chopped bacon or prosciutto ham
- 6 tbsp. grated Romano cheese
- 2 eggs, beaten
- ¼ tsp. salt
- ¼ tsp. white pepper
- 2 cups seasoned breadcrumbs
- 3 tbsp. butter
- 3 tbsp. olive oil
- 6 oz. white wine
- 1 lb. Roma tomatoes, peeled, seeded and chopped
- 1 tsp. crushed oregano
- 3 garlic cloves, peeled and slivered
- 1 tbsp. balsamic vinegar

> SERVE THE QUENELLES
> OVER BUTTERED NOODLES
> AS AN ENTRÉE OR IN A
> CHAFING DISH AS AN
> HORS D'OEUVRE.

DIRECTIONS

In a large bowl, mix together the venison, bacon or prosciutto, cheese, salt, and pepper. Using a tablespoon, shape the mixture into quenelles (tear-dropped shaped) and coat in breadcrumbs.

In a large skillet, heat the butter and olive oil and brown the quenelles on all sides. Transfer to a holding pan and keep warm. Add the wine to the skillet, stir in the tomatoes, oregano, garlic and vinegar. Heat to almost boiling. Add the quenelles and heat through.

VENISON POCKET

SERVES 8

INGREDIENTS

- 1½ lb. ground venison
- ½ lb. bulk pork sausage, breakfast or Italian
- ½ cup ketchup
- 1 cup seasoned breadcrumbs
- 1 large egg, beaten
- 2 large carrots, peeled and sliced
- 2–3 medium potatoes, sliced
- 2 onions, sliced
- 16 tbsp. butter, softened
- 8 12"x20" pieces aluminum foil

DIRECTIONS

In a medium bowl, mix together the venison and sausage. Add the breadcrumbs, ketchup and egg. Mix well and form into 8 patties.

Butter ½ of the foil sheet. Place 5–6 slices potato on the buttered portion of the foil. Top the potatoes with a venison patty, several onion slices and a butter pat. Fold the foil over the top and fold the edges to seal. Place packets on a cookie sheet and bake in a 325 degree oven for 60 minutes.

YOU CAN PREPARE THESE PACKETS AND
FREEZE FOR LATER USE. IF BAKING FROM
FROZEN, ADD 15 MINUTES TO BAKING TIME.

VENISON WITH BLACKBEANS AND RICE

 SERVES 6–8

INGREDIENTS

- 1 lb. ground venison
- ½ cup olive oil
- 1 large onion, peeled, sliced and chopped
- 1 green pepper, seeded, sliced and chopped
- 1 red pepper, seeded, sliced and chopped
- 1 jalapeño pepper, seeded, sliced and chopped
- 1 15-oz. can sliced stewed tomatoes
- 2 15-oz. cans black beans
- 1 tbsp. minced garlic (4 cloves)
- 1½ tsp. oregano
- 1 tsp. ground cumin
- 1 tbsp. brown sugar
- 1 tbsp. red wine vinegar
- ½ cup red wine
- 3 tbsp. olive oil
- 2 tsp. salt (optional)

THIS MAKES A DELICIOUS BUFFET DISH. PLACE IN AN OVENPROOF CASSEROLE DISH, TOP WITH CHEESE AND BAKE UNTIL HOT AND BUBBLY.

DIRECTIONS

Heat a 4-quart stockpot over medium heat. Add ½ cup olive oil and ground venison, stirring until browned. Stir in the onion and peppers and cook until vegetables are soft, 3–5 minutes.

In a large bowl, mix together the wine, 3 tablespoons olive oil, garlic, oregano, cumin, brown sugar and red wine vinegar. Add to the venison mixture and stir in the stewed tomatoes and black beans. Reduce heat to low and cook for 15 minutes. Serve over steamed white rice.

VENISON QUATTRO FORMAGGIO

SERVES 8

INGREDIENTS

- 2 lbs. ground venison
- 3 tbsp. olive oil
- 2 carrots, peeled, sliced and finely chopped
- 3 stalks celery, sliced and finely chopped
- 1 medium onion, cut into ¼" dice
- 2 tsp. minced garlic
- 2 eggs, beaten
- 3 cups seasoned breadcrumbs
- ¼ cup fresh minced parsley
- 4 oz. shredded asiago cheese
- 4 oz. shredded provolone cheese
- 4 oz. shredded cheddar cheese
- 2 oz. grated Parmesan cheese
- ⅛ tsp. crushed dried thyme
- ½ tsp. white pepper
- 1 tsp. salt

THE HUMBLE MEATLOAF
TRANSFORMED INTO A
GOURMET DINNER.

DIRECTIONS

In a heavy skillet or sauté pan over medium heat, sauté the carrots, celery and onion in olive oil for 10 minutes. Stir in the garlic during the last minute. Remove from heat and allow to cool.

In a large bowl, combine the breadcrumbs with the cheeses, salt, pepper and thyme. In another large bowl, add ⅔ of the breadcrumb cheese mixture, parsley, venison, eggs and the cooled vegetables. Combine and thoroughly mix by hand. Transfer to a nonstick baking dish and form into a loaf 9x4". Coat top and sides with the remaining breadcrumbs and cheese. Bake in a 325 degree oven about 1 hour or until the internal temperature reaches 160–180 degrees.

STUFFED ACORN SQUASH

SERVES 6-8

INGREDIENTS

- 1½ lb. ground venison
- 2 slices bread soaked in ¼ cup milk
- 1 small onion, peeled, sliced and minced
- 1 small green bell pepper, seeded, sliced and minced
- 1 tbsp. onion soup mix
- ¼ tsp. granulated garlic
- 2 eggs, beaten
- 3–4 acorn squash

SAUCE

- 1 can condensed tomato soup
- ½ cup cranberry juice
- ½ cup heavy cream
- 1 tsp. hot sauce or a few drops of tabasco

FOR A SMALLER PORTION, CUT THE SQUASH INTO
2 1/2 THICK SLICES. REMOVE THE SEEDS AND FILL
THE HOLE WITH THE VENISON MIXTURE. PLACE IN
A BUTTERED BAKING DISH AND OMIT THE WATER.
REDUCE BAKING TIME TO 15-20 MINUTES.

DIRECTIONS

Preheat oven to 325 degrees.

In a large stainless steel bowl, combine the venison, onion, green pepper, onion soup mix and granulated garlic. Add the milk-soaked bread and the eggs and mix thoroughly by hand.

Cut the squash in half lengthwise. Remove the seeds and season lightly with salt and pepper. Divide the venison mixture equally to fill the squash halves.

Place the squash in a deep baking pan. Add ½" water. Cover with foil and bake 45 minutes to 1 hour or until the squash is soft and tender. Remove the foil and place a teaspoon of butter on each squash half. Return to the oven, uncovered, for 15 minutes.

To make the sauce: In a 1½ quart saucepan, add the condensed soup and, over medium heat, whisk in the cranberry juice, cream and hot sauce. Whisk until slightly thickened. Plate the squash and serve the sauce on the side.

MISCELLANEOUS VENISON RECIPES

CACCIATORE

INGREDIENTS
- **2–3 lbs. boneless venison, sliced ½" thick and tenderized with a meat mallet**

SEASONED FLOUR
- **1 cup flour**
- **½ tsp. white pepper**
- **½ tsp. salt**
- **½ tsp. crushed oregano**
- **½ tsp. thyme**
- **⅓ cup olive oil**
- **1 large onion, peeled, sliced and cut in half**
- **1 tsp. minced garlic, about 2 cloves**
- **1 green bell pepper, seeded and cut in strips**
- **1 red bell pepper, seeded and cut in strips**
- **½ lb. button mushrooms, cut in half**
- **2 medium zucchini squash, sliced ⅔" thick**
- **1 15-oz. can tomato purée**
- **1 cup red wine**

> YOU CAN PREPARE THIS DISH A DAY OR TWO AHEAD OF SERVING. DON'T ADD THE ZUCCHINI AND MUSHROOMS UNTIL YOU ARE REHEATING THE DISH.

DIRECTIONS
Cut the steak crosswise into uniform serving portions. Place the seasoned flour in a large plastic bag. Place the venison, 4 or 5 pieces at a time, in the bag and shake to coat. Remove venison to holding tray.

In a large sauté pan, heat ½ of the olive oil and brown the venison on both sides. Remove the venison and keep warm.

Add remaining oil to the sauté pan. Add the garlic, onion, and peppers and brown quickly. Add the tomatoes, red wine and venison. Cover and simmer 20–30 minutes until the venison is tender. Add the zucchini and mushrooms. Simmer, covered, 10–15 minutes. Remove the cover and cook an additional 10 minutes or until sauce is somewhat reduced. Serve over your favorite pasta.

FARMHOUSE VENISON

SERVES 6–8

INGREDIENTS

2 lb. venison, cut into 1" cubes
1 tsp. seasoned salt
½ tsp. white pepper
1 tsp. paprika
1 cup ketchup
2 medium zucchini, cut into 1" slices
2 medium yellow squash, cut into 1" slices
2 cups chicken stock
1 can whole kernel corn
2 tbsp. cornstarch
3 tbsp. water

DIRECTIONS

Season the venison with the salt, pepper and paprika. Place in a slow cooker with the chicken stock and ketchup. Cover and cook on low 6–8 hours or until venison is fork tender. Increase heat to high, stir in corn, zucchini and yellow squash. Dissolve the cornstarch in the water and stir into the meat mixture in the slow cooker. Continue cooking for 10–20 minutes until thickened.

THIS IS A GREAT MEAL TO MAKE A DAY OR TWO
AHEAD. JUST REHEAT IN THE MICROWAVE AND
SERVE OVER WIDE EGG NOODLES.

FINNISH VENISON AND PORK

SERVES 6–8

INGREDIENTS

- 1 lb. boneless venison, cut into 1" cubes
- 1 lb. boneless pork, cut into 1" cubes
- ½ cup dried cranberries
- 1½ cup white wine
- ½ cup port wine
- ⅓ cup olive oil
- ¼ cup butter
- ¼ lb. bacon, chopped
- 1 large onion, peeled, sliced and chopped
- ½ lb. button mushrooms, sliced
- 1½ cups chicken stock
- 1 cup heavy cream

FOR A TOUCH OF OLD WORLD FLAVOR, ADD A PINCH OF FRESHLY GRATED NUTMEG TO THE FINISHED SAUCE.

DIRECTIONS

Place venison, pork and dried cranberries in a stainless steel bowl. Add the white wine and port wine and stir well. Cover with plastic wrap and refrigerate overnight.

Drain the wine from the meat and fruit, reserving the liquid. Separate the meat from the cranberries. Dry the meat on paper towels.

Using a heavy dutch oven, heat ½ of the butter and ½ of the olive oil. Brown the venison and pork in small batches, adding butter and olive oil as needed. Add the bacon and onion and cook on low until the onion is opaque. Return the venison and pork to the dutch oven. Add the reserved liquid and the chicken stock. Bring to a boil. Stir in the cranberries. Reduce heat to low, cover and simmer 20–30 minutes or until the meat is tender.

Remove 1 cup cooking liquid and mix with the heavy cream. Stir into the meat mixture and heat thoroughly. Adjust seasoning to taste with salt and pepper. Serve over boiled potatoes or wide egg noodles.

SATÉ

SERVES 4–6

INGREDIENTS
- 1 lb. venison, thinly sliced and cut into strips 1"
  wide and 2–3" long 6" bamboo skewers

MARINADE
- 2 cloves garlic, minced
- 1 small onion, sliced and minced
- 1 tbsp. brown sugar
- Juice of 1 lime
- 1 tbsp. fish sauce
- 1 tsp. red thai curry paste, dissolved
  in 2 tbsp. teriyaki sauce
- 1 tbsp. sesame oil

TAKE THE TIME TO VISIT
AN ORIENTAL GROCERY
AND PURCHASE AT LEAST
3 TYPES OF CURRY PASTE
(PANANG, YELLOW
AND RED).

PEANUT DIPPING SAUCE
- ½ cup peanut butter
- ½ cup mayonnaise
- 1 tbsp. brown sugar
- 1 tbsp. red thai curry paste, dissolved in 2 tbsp. hot water
- 1 tbsp. teriyaki sauce

DIRECTIONS
Combine all marinade ingredients in a food processor and process with a
steel blade until smooth. Place in a large stainless steel bowl with venison
strips. Cover and refrigerate overnight.

Preheat oven to 325 degrees.

Thread venison strips lengthwise onto the bamboo skewers, 2 pieces per
skewer. Place on a nonstick sheet pan or a cookie sheet sprayed with oil and
bake for 10–12 minutes, basting with the marinade at 5 minute intervals.

In a bowl, whisk together the dipping sauce ingredients. Arrange the saté
skewers on a serving platter around a bowl of the peanut dipping sauce.

RACK OF VENISON

SERVES 2–4

INGREDIENTS
- 1 8-bone rack of venison
- 2 tbsp. lemon juice

DRY RUB MIX
- 1 tsp. crushed oregano
- ½ tsp. crushed marjoram
- ¼ tsp. sea salt
- ¼ tsp. granulated garlic
- ¼ tsp. dried lemon peel, ground
- ¼ tsp. dried orange peel, ground
- 1/8 tsp. white pepper
- 1/8 tsp. black pepper

USE THE SAME DRY RUB ON CHICKEN OR LAMB. FOR ADDED FLAVOR, BASTE DURING BAKING WITH GARLIC BUTTER AND LEMON JUICE.

DIRECTIONS
Mix together all dry rub ingredients in a food processor. Process for 10 seconds.

Moisten the venison rack with lemon juice and dust with the dry rub. Cover and let sit for 30 minutes. Heat a gas or charcoal grill to medium-high. Cook the venison for 3 minutes on a side. Place venison in a baking dish and roast in a 350 degree oven for 15 minutes. Let the venison sit loosely covered for 10 minutes before carving.

SWEET SOUR VENISON

INGREDIENTS

- 2 lb. boneless venison, sliced ½" thick and cut into ¼" strips
- ¼ cup cornstarch
- ⅓ cup teriyaki sauce
- 2 tbsp. vegetable oil
- 1 tsp. minced garlic
- 1 green bell pepper, seeded and cut into strips
- 1 medium onion, peeled, sliced and cut in half
- 2 medium carrots, peeled and sliced diagonally
- 1 tbsp. cornstarch
- 2 tbsp. sugar
- 2 tbsp. ketchup
- ¼ cup teriyaki sauce
- 2 tbsp. lemon juice
- ⅛ tsp. toasted sesame seeds
- ½ tbsp. sesame oil
- 1 8-oz. can pineapple chunks, drained

ADD A FEW DROPS OF TABASCO TO HEAT UP THE SAUCE.

DIRECTIONS

In a medium size bowl, whisk together the ¼ cup cornstarch and ⅓ cup teriyaki sauce. Add the venison and toss to coat. Let sit at least 5 minutes.

In a wok or large skillet, heat the oil. Remove the venison from the marinade with a slotted spoon and stir-fry until brown. Remove venison from the wok. Stir-fry the vegetables for 3–5 minutes or until tender crisp. Return the venison to the wok. Whisk together 1 tablespoon cornstarch, sugar, ketchup, lemon juice, ¼ cup teriyaki sauce, sesame seeds and sesame oil. Add to venison mixture in the wok and simmer 3–5 minutes or until thickened. Stir in the pineapple and heat until bubbly. Serve over steamed white or brown rice.

VENISON BROCCOLI STIR-FRY

INGREDIENTS

- 1 lb. broccoli, trimmed, peeled and sliced diagonally
- 2 tbsp. vegetable oil
- 2 tsp. minced garlic (3 cloves)
- 8 oz. venison, cut 2" thick and sliced thin across the grain
- 1 large onion, sliced and quartered
- 1 medium red bell pepper, seeded and cut into strips
- Oriental noodles or steamed rice
- Stir Fry Sauce

STIR FRY SAUCE

Mix together:
- 3 tbsp. oyster sauce
- 3 tbsp. teriyaki sauce
- 1 tsp. cornstarch
- 1 tsp. brown sugar

DIRECTIONS

Blanch broccoli in boiling water until bright green, 2–3 minutes.

Heat a wok or heavy skillet. In 1 tablespoon vegetable oil, sauté the garlic approximately 1 minute. Add venison, broccoli and onion. Stir fry about 3 minutes. Add the bell pepper and stir-fry sauce. Cover and cook until all vegetables are tender crisp.

Serve over noodles or rice.

THE STIR-FRY SAUCE STORES WELL UNDER
REFRIGERATION. IF YOU LIKE IT SPICY, ADD
1/4 TABLESPOON RED PEPPER FLAKES.

VENISON CURRY

INGREDIENTS

- 2 lbs. boneless venison, cut into bite-sized pieces
- 2 tbsp. olive oil
- 2 tbsp. yellow curry paste, dissolved in ⅓ cup hot water
- 1 tbsp. sesame oil
- 2 cups chicken stock
- 1 15-oz. can unsweetened coconut milk
- ½ cup lentils
- 2 tbsp. butter
- 2 medium onions, sliced into thick rings
- 1 cup cauliflower florets (about 6 oz.)
- 1 cup broccoli florets (about 6 oz.)
- 1 cup sliced carrot
- 1 cup sliced celery

KEEP SOME OF THIS DISH IN THE FREEZER FOR A QUICK MEAL OR FOR THOSE DROP-IN DINNER GUESTS.

DIRECTIONS

In a heavy 6-quart dutch oven, heat the olive oil over medium-high heat. Brown the venison on all sides in several batches. Return all venison to the dutch oven and add the dissolved curry paste, sesame oil, chicken stock and coconut milk. Reduce heat to medium. Cover and cook until venison is tender. Stir in lentils. Cover and continue cooking another 20–30 minutes.

In a large skillet or sauté pan, melt the butter over low heat. Add the onions, broccoli, cauliflower, carrot and celery. Increase heat to medium and cook until the onions are browned. Add 1 cup of the cooking stock, bring to a boil. Reduce heat and simmer uncovered for 5 minutes.

Add vegetables to the venison. Simmer over medium heat until the vegetables are tender, about 30 minutes. Serve over steamed rice.

ITALIAN VENISON CUTLETS
WITH ARTICHOKE HEARTS

SERVES 6-8

INGREDIENTS

- 1½ lb. boneless venison leg, sliced ⅜" thick
- 4 tbsp. olive oil
- 2 eggs, beaten
- ½ cup flour
- ¼ tsp. salt
- ¼ tsp. white pepper
- ⅛ tsp. granulated garlic
- ⅓ cup chicken stock
- 1 package frozen artichoke hearts, thawed and drained
- 3 tbsp. butter
- ½ tsp. sea salt
- ¼ cup grated Parmesan cheese
- ¼ cup shredded asiago cheese

ADD ZUCCHINI AND TOMATOES AND A SPRINKLING OF OREGANO FOR ADDITIONAL FLAVORS.

DIRECTIONS

Using an ovenproof deep skillet or sauté pan, melt the butter and sauté the artichokes 5–6 minutes. Sprinkle with sea salt and remove from pan.

Flatten the venison cutlets between 2 sheets of waxed paper until ½ the original thickness. Dip the venison in egg, then in a mixture of flour, salt, pepper and garlic.

In a large skillet. Heat the oil over low heat and brown the venison on both sides. Transfer to the ovenproof deep skillet. Distribute the artichokes evenly over the venison cutlets. Add the chicken stock and top with the cheeses. Bake in a 325 degree oven for 15 minutes or until the cheese is bubbly.

INDEX

Aussie Marinated Venison 26

Basque Stew 45

Bayou Venison 48

BBQ Venison Chops with Wild Rice
	Pancakes 50–51

Berliner Venison and Sauerkraut 43

Breaded Venison Chops 49

Breakfast Dishes
	Breakfast Skillet 92
	Venison Breakfast Wrap 93

Breakfast Skillet 92

Breakfast Wrap 93

Burgers with Bacon and Cheddar 94

Cacciatore 128

Camp Stew 28–29

Carolina BBQ 52–53

Casseroles
	Berliner Venison and Sauerkraut 44
	Hunting Camp Italian Casserole 31
	Mashed Potato, Venison and Spinach
		Pie 32–33
	Southwestern Casserole 27
	Texas Venison and Beans 37
	Spanish Ragout of Venison 38–39
	Venison and Wild Rice Gumbo 30

Chicken Fried Venison Steak 54–55

Chilis
	Hot Chili 19

Venison Chili with Chorizo Sausage 21

Venison Chili with Italian Sausage 22

Chops
	BBQ Venison Chops with Wild Rice
		Pancakes 50–51
	Breaded Venison Chops 49
	Coriander and Honey Glazed Venison
Chops 68
	Lemon Venison Chops 57
	Venison Chops and Sausage with
		Sauerkraut 72

Chowder
	Spicy Venison and Corn Chowder 20

Coriander and Honey Glazed Venison
	Chops 68

Farmhouse Venison 129

Finnish Venison and Pork 130

Frittata 96–97

German Style Ground Venison 95

Goulash Soup 18

Ground Venison
	Breakfast Skillet 92
	Burgers with Bacon and Cheddar 94
	Frittata 96–97
	German Style Ground Venison 95
	Individual Meatloaves 98
	Italian Meatballs 99
	Konigsberger Klopse (German

Meatballs) 100–101
Meatloaf a la Reuben 102
Meatloaf 103
Mostaciolli 104
Quick Stroganoff 105
Ragout 106
Spaghetti Sauce 107
Spicy Venison and Eggplant 108
Stuffed Acorn Squash 124
Stuffed Burgers 109
Stuffed Peppers 112
Gumbo
  Venison and Wild Rice Casserole 30
Gumbo
  Venison and Wild Rice Casserole 30
Gumbo
  Venison and Wild Rice Casserole 30
Hamburger Meat
  Breakfast Skillet 92
  Burgers with Bacon and Cheddar 94
  Frittata 96–97
  German Style Ground Venison 95
  Individual Meatloaves 98
  Italian Meatballs 99
  Konigsberger Klopse (German
    Meatballs) 100–101
  Meatloaf ala Reuben 102
  Mostaciolli 104
  Quick Stroganoff 105
  Ragout 106
  Spaghetti Sauce 107
  Spicy Venison and Eggplant 108
  Stuffed Acorn Squash 124
  Stuffed Burgers 109
  Stuffed Peppers 112
  Sweet Sour Stuffed Cabbage 113
  Thai Country–Style Curry 114
  Thai Meatballs 115
  Venison BBQ
  Venison with Blackbeans and Rice 122
  Venison Breakfast Wrap 93
  Venison and Cornbread Pie 118–119

Venison Dumplings Bolognese 120
Venison Pocket 121
Venison Quattro Fromaggio 123
Venison and Spanish Rice 116
Venison Turban 110–111
Hot Chili 19
Hungarian Venison Paprikash 85
Hunting Camp Italian Casserole 31
Individual Meatloaves 98
Introduction 9–10
  Sweet Sour Stuffed Cabbage 113
  Thai Country–Style Curry 114
  Thai Meatballs 115
  Venison BBQ 117
  Venison with Blackbeans and Rice 122
  Venison Breakfast Wrap 93
  Venison and Cornbread Pie 118–119
  Venison Dumplings Bolognese 120
  Venison Pocket 121
  Venison Quattro Fromaggio 123
  Venison and Spanish Rice
  Venison Turban 110–111
Italian Meatballs 99
Italian Venison Cutlets with Artichoke
Hearts 136
Konigsberger Klopse (German Meatballs)
    100–101
Leftover Venison Soup 15
Lemon Venison Chops 57
Mashed Potato, Venison and Spinach
    Pie 32–33
Meatballs
  Italian Meatballs 99
  Konigsberger Klopse (German
    Meatballs) 100–101
  Thai Meatballs 115
Meatloaf 103
Meatloaves
  Individual Meatloaves 98
  Meatloaf ala Reuben 102
  Meatloaf 103
Meatloaf ala Reuben 103

Meat Pie
    Mashed Potato, Venison and Spinach
        Pie 32–33
    Venison and Cornbread Pie 118–119
Mediterranean Venison 86
Moroccan Stew 34
Mostaciolli 104
Mother Mary's Venison Stew 35
Mustard Herb Venison 36
New England Venison Roast 75
Pot–au–Feu For Two 58–59
Quick Stroganoff 105
Rack of Venison 132
Ragout 106
Ragouts
    Ragout 106
    Spanish Ragout of Venison 38–39
Rheinischer Stuffed Venison Roast 60
Ribs
    Rack of Venison 132
Roasts
    Bayou Venison 48
    Cacciatore 128
    Carolina BBQ 52–53
    Farmhouse Venison 129
    Finnish Venison and Pork 130
    Italian Venison Cutlets with Artichoke
Hearts 136
    New England Venison Roast 75
    Rheinischer Stuffed Venison Roast 60
    Roast Venison with Apricots, Prunes
        and Pears 62–63
    Saurbraten 64–65
    Sate' 131
    South of the Border Venison 67
    Sweet Sour Venison 133
    Thai Curry 70
    Venison Broccoli Stir Fry 134
    Venison Curry 135
    Venison Fajitas 84
    Venison with Peppers and Pea Pods 77
    Venison Shoulder Roast with Apples,

Turnips and Carrots 73
    Venison Shoulder Roast with Bread
Stuffing 88–89
    Venison, Very Dry with an Olive 79
    Venison with Zinfandel and Dried
        Cranberries 80–81
    Warsaw Venison 61
Roast Venison with Apricots, Prunes
    and Pears 62–63
Roast Venison Loin ala Frankfurt 82
Sate' 131
Sauerbraten 64–65
Soups
    Goulash Soup 18
    Hot Chili 19
    Leftover Venison Soup 15
    Spicy Venison and Corn Chowder 20
    Thai Venison Shank Soup 16–17
    Venison Chili with Chorizo Sausage 21
    Venison Chili with Italian Sausage 22
    Venison Soup 14
South of the Border Venison 67
Southwestern Casserole 27
Spaghetti Sauce 107
Spanish Ragout of Venison 38–39
Spicy Venison and Corn Chowder 20
Spicy Venison and Eggplant 108
Steak au Poivre 56
Steaks
    Cacciatore 128
    Chicken Fried Venison Steak 54–55
    Farmhouse Venison 129
    Finnish Venison and Pork 130
    Hungarian Venison Paprikash 85
    Mediterranean Venison 86
    Pot–au–Feu for Two 58–59
    Roast Venison Loin ala Frankfurt 82
    Saté 131
    Steak au Poivre 56
    Sweet Sour Venison 133
    Szechuan Venison with Dried
        Cranberries in Port Wine 69

Teriyaki Venison 71
Thai Curry 70
Venison Broccoli Stir Fry 134
Venison Curry 135
Venison Medallions with Port Wine
    and Lingonberries 83
Venison with Peppers and Pasta 76
Venison with Peppers and Pea Pods 77
Venison Piccata 74
Venison Rouladen 78
Venison Schnitzel 66
Venison Stroganoff 87
Stews
    Aussie Marinated Venison 26
    Basque Stew 45
    Camp Stew 28–29
    Moroccan Stew 34
    Mother Mary's Venison Stew 35
    Mustard Herb Venison 36
    Venison Burgundy 40
    Venison Stew Parnassus 41
    Venison Stew with Squash 42
    Venison Stew 43
Stuffed Acorn Squash 124
Stuffed Burgers 109
Stuffed Peppers 112
Sweet Sour Stuffed Cabbage 113
Sweet Sour Venison 133
Szechuan Venison with Dried Cranberries
    in Port Wine 69
Teriyaki Venison 71
Texas Venison and Beans 37
Thai Country Style Curry 114
Thai Curry
Thai Meatballs 115
Thai Venison Shank Soup 16–17
Venison BBQ 117
Venison with Blackbeans and Rice
Venison Breakfast Wrap 93
Venison Broccoli Stir Fry 134
Venison Burgundy 40
Venison Chili with Chorizo Sausage 21

Venison Chili with Italian Sausage 22
Venison Chops and Sausage with
    Sauerkraut 72
Venison and Cornbread Pie 118–119
Venison Curry 135
Venison Dumplings Bolognese 120
Venison Fajitas 84
Venison Medallions with Port Wine and
Lingonberries 83
Venison with Peppers and Pasta 76
Venison with Peppers and Pea Pods 77
Venison Piccata 74
Venison Pocket 121
Venison Quattro Formaggio 123
Venison Rouladen 78
Venison Schnitzel 66
Venison Shoulder Roast with Apples,
    Turnips and Carrots 73
Venison Shoulder Roast with Bread
    Stuffing 88–89
Venison Soup 14
Venison and Spanish Rice 116
Venison Stew Parnassus 41
Venison Stew with Squash 43
Venison Stew 43
Venison Stroganoff 87
Venison Turban 110–111
Venison, Very Dry with an Olive 79
Venison and Wild Rice Gumbo 30
Venison with Zinfandel and Dried
    Cranberries 80–81
Warsaw Venison 61